ODD TYPE
WRITERS

ODD TYPE WRITERS

From Joyce and Dickens
to Wharton and Welty,
the Obsessive Habits
and Quirky Techniques
of Great Authors

Celia Blue Johnson

A PERIGEE BOOK

A PERIGEE BOOK
Published by the Penguin Group
Penguin Group (USA) Inc.
375 Hudson Street, New York, New York 10014, USA

USA I Canada I UK I Ireland I Australia I New Zealand I India I South Africa I China

Penguin Books Ltd., Registered Offices: 80 Strand, London WC2R 0RL, England
For more information about the Penguin Group, visit penguin.com.

Library of Congress Cataloging-in-Publication Data

Johnson, Celia Blue.
Odd type writers : from Joyce and Dickens to Wharton and Welty, the obsessive habits
and quirky techniques of great authors / Celia Blue Johnson.
pages cm
"A Perigee book."
Includes bibliographical references and index.
ISBN 978-0-399-15994-7 (pbk.)
1. Authorship—Miscellanea.   2. Authorship—Anecdotes.   I. Title.
PN165.J64   2013
808'02—dc23   2013002340

First edition: June 2013

PRINTED IN THE UNITED STATES OF AMERICA

10   9   8   7   6   5   4   3   2   1

Text design by Laura K. Corless

Most Perigee books are available at special quantity discounts for bulk purchases for sales
promotions, premiums, fund-raising, or educational use. Special books, or book excerpts,
can also be created to fit specific needs. For details, write: Special.Markets@us.penguingroup.com.

FOR IAN

Contents

CONTENTS

CONTENTS

ODD TYPE WRITERS

Introduction

The first time I visited Chumley's,* I got lost on the way. It was early evening, and it had been snowing all afternoon. By the time I emerged from the Christopher Street subway stop, the sidewalks were covered in a thick layer of white. Streetlights and neon signs illuminated falling snowflakes. Pedestrians strolled and strode, some slipping on patches of slick ground. I turned onto one of the winding streets that led into the heart of Manhattan's West Village, and suddenly the bustle of Seventh Avenue disappeared. It was still and quiet. I could hear my own muffled footsteps as I trudged through the snow.

Unlike much of Manhattan, the streets in the West Village have no apparent order. They form a confusing maze

---

* Unfortunately, Chumley's closed after suffering structural damage in 2007. Literary fans still eagerly await the reopening of this historic hot spot.

for anyone who, like me, isn't familiar with the area. I accordingly took several wrong turns before finally landing on Bedford Street. Then I must have walked past Chumley's three or four times before I spotted the numbers on the door. The trouble is that the building looked like every other charming brick home in the area. But, then again, that was the point. As a speakeasy during Prohibition, Chumley's was supposed to blend in. Later, when the ban on alcohol was lifted, the owner of the establishment decided to stick with a nondescript façade.

There was no mistaking the longtime literary hub once I walked inside. People crowded in the entryway, waiting for spots to open up. Waiters bobbed and weaved between tables, carrying pints of beer and hearty fare. Lively conversations, cackles, clinking glasses, and upbeat music all blended into a constant roar. Between the body heat and the flames jumping in an open fireplace, the restaurant was nice and toasty. This was a world apart from the cold, sleepy street beyond the front door.

The walls were filled with photographs of writers who had frequented Chumley's over the years. Hundreds of book covers wound through the pub below the portraits. F. Scott Fitzgerald, John Steinbeck, J. D. Salinger, and Edna St. Vincent Millay are just a few of the literary legends who sat at the wooden tables and imbibed. The familiar faces in the black-and-white photos smiled mischievously or stared off into the distance. They appeared to be only briefly frozen in time. It was as though they might, at any moment, chime in on a joke or a serious discussion. Imagine catching a witty retort from James Thurber or Dorothy Parker!

Those people are long gone, but the shadows of their lives dip back to this one place. When my name was called and I slid into a booth, I closed my eyes for a few seconds. Voices ebbed and flowed around me. I imagined that a deep laugh burst from Ernest Hemingway rather than a stranger at the next table. From across the room, I could make out an excited voice, talking too rapidly for me to catch exactly what was said. That, I thought, could have been Jack Kerouac. Of course, there's no way to re-create the banter between the brilliant minds who crowded into Chumley's. And yet, sitting there, it crossed my mind that this is about as close as it gets.

Walking into a legendary writer's home has been an altogether different experience for me. There tends to be a hallowed hush within the walls. Important rooms are roped off, understandably to preserve the space. One can peer into an author's study, but not sit in the same spot where she or he wrote. Geographically, it's a small difference, standing inside or outside a room. But it's significant. From the doorway, I find it difficult to conjure anything more than a one-dimensional picture of a writer sitting at a desk. In Chumley's it felt as though I had been transported to another time. As a literary enthusiast, I seek that immediacy and intimacy. In part, that's why I wrote this book. I wanted to animate those eerily quiet rooms where famous people composed their groundbreaking works.

If you're a bookworm, then it's likely you've curled up with a novel by at least one of the authors featured in *Odd Type Writers*. After opening to page one, hours may have slipped by before you thought to look up. That power to mesmerize has an intangible, almost magical quality, one I wouldn't dare to try and meddle with by attempting to define it. It was never my goal as I wrote this book to discover what made literary geniuses tick. The nuances of any mind are impossible to pinpoint.

In *Odd Type Writers*, I simply wanted to envision a study as it was when a writer was in it. I wanted to know: typewriter, pencil, or pen? Desk chair, armchair, or couch? Was the furniture selection based on practical or sentimental reasons? Perhaps a cat purred nearby. Maybe a window was propped open so fresh air could wash into the room. I certainly didn't expect to find more than small distinctions that set one writer apart from another. I had no idea that I was about to venture into such strange literary territory.

It turns out that writers are a very quirky bunch. As I pored over books and clicked from one website to the next, I stumbled across surprisingly odd facts about renowned authors and their work habits. I was shocked to discover that Friedrich Schiller dipped his feet in cold water to help him stay awake. I found it hard to believe that James Joyce wrote in crayon on pieces of cardboard, and yet that's how he composed *Ulysses* and *Finnegans Wake*. When I discovered that Colette picked fleas from her pets before picking up her pen, I almost dropped my book. These techniques seemed more outlandish than the most far-fetched fiction.

I also discovered unusually obsessive behavior. There were authors who clung to habits that, at first glance, seemed standard. For example, Flannery O'Connor fixed a particular time to write. Jack London set a daily quota of words. It was their steadfast adherence to these practices that set them apart from the norm. O'Connor woke up early to work every morning, even on weekends, without allocating any time off. London wrote a thousand words a day, every day, throughout his entire career. To me, this spirited obsession was just as singular as more immediately shocking practices.

I collected the most interesting quirks and obsessions that I came across, and wrote about them in this book. Many of these oddities are listed anecdotally in articles, but I strove to describe each one in a fuller scope. In each essay about a specific author, I explored the peculiar work habits within the context of his or her career. I wanted to know when quirks originated, how long they lasted, and whether one habit was exchanged for another. I wanted to rustle up authors' descriptions of their own quirks, whether they were discussed in interviews, mentioned in letters, or referred to in diary entries.

I did not follow a straight line from start to finish as I put together this book. I took detours, stumbling upon one fact that led to a related fact that led to a different author and an altogether different fact. These offshoots inspired me to write the short miscellaneous compilations you'll find throughout the book. These compilation essays pull together disparate authors beneath the umbrella of a quirk they all shared.

In conducting research for *Odd Type Writers*, I sifted through letters, memoirs, articles, and biographies. First- and secondhand accounts revealed fascinating details about writers' habits. Some authors described their work process in letters or conversations. Others were more tight-lipped about their methods. In those cases, I relied on accounts from friends, family members, and colleagues.

One must always keep in mind that these writers and the people around them may have, at some point, embellished the facts. Quirks are great fodder for gossip and can morph into gross exaggeration when passed from one person to the next. There's also no way to escape self-mythologizing, particularly when dealing with some of the greatest storytellers that ever lived. Yet even when authors stretch the truth, they reveal something about themselves, whether it is the desire to project a certain image or the need to shy away from one. So I proceeded cautiously as I assembled my research, referencing several sources and noting when one account contradicted another.

In *Odd Type Writers*, you will discover a wide variety of peculiar habits that were adopted by great writers. Edgar

Allan Poe balanced a cat on his shoulder while he wrote. Agatha Christie munched on apples in her bathtub while concocting murder plots. Victor Hugo shut himself inside and wore nothing but a long, gray, knitted shawl when he was on a tight deadline. Friedrich Schiller filled his desk drawer with rotten apples, relying on the pungent smell to spark his creativity. You could adopt one of these practices or, more ambitiously, combine several of them, and chances are you still wouldn't invoke genius. These tales don't hold a secret formula for writing a great novel. Rather, the authors in this book prove that the path to great literature is paved with one's own eccentricities rather than someone else's.

Virginia Woolf once wrote, "A woman must have money and a room of her own to write fiction." I've read Woolf's essay, "A Room of One's Own," in which this line appears, many times. But until I embarked on this literary expedition, I didn't fully realize the significance of a room. Truly a writer needs space. A room is far more than four walls, a ceiling, and a door. It's is a place where an author can embrace, and even harness, her or his idiosyncrasies. In the solitude of a room, a writer's creativity manifests not only on the page, but also in unique work habits.

Odd Type Writers leads you through the places where famous authors worked. Many of them contain strange props, like rotten apples, ashtrays with no more than three cigarettes, and bowls of ice cream. You'll discover that some writers clung to a specific location, a place they could adapt to fit their needs. For other writers, a room was more of a metaphor, something to be carried from one location to the next, or even over a threshold and into the wilderness. In each space, you'll have a chance to witness an extraordinary writer at work. I'm sure you'll find that they are an odd, courageous lot. These writers boldly set stories to paper in unique and surprising ways, whether that meant scrawling in crayon, composing in purple ink, or speaking into a Dictaphone.

Rotten Ideas

FRIEDRICH SCHILLER

1759–1805

An air beneficial to Schiller acted on me like poison.

—Johann Wolfgang von Goethe,
in conversation with Johann Peter Eckermann

According to Johann Wolfgang von Goethe, he and Friedrich Schiller were direct opposites, right down to their writing habits. He reminisced about their differences with biographer Johann Peter Eckermann a couple of decades after Schiller's death. Goethe described a particularly strange incident that reflected how unalike they were. He had dropped by Schiller's home and, after finding that his friend was out, decided to wait for him to return. Rather than wasting a few spare moments, the productive poet sat down at Schiller's desk to jot down a few notes. Then a peculiar stench prompted Goethe to pause. Somehow, an oppressive odor had infiltrated the room.

Goethe followed the odor to its origin, which was actually right by where he sat. It was emanating from a drawer in Schiller's desk. Goethe leaned down, opened the drawer, and found a pile of rotten apples. The smell was so overpowering that he became light-headed. He walked to the window and breathed in a few good doses of fresh air. Goethe was naturally curious about the trove of trash, though Schiller's wife, Charlotte, could only offer the strange truth: Schiller had deliberately let the apples spoil. The aroma, somehow, inspired him, and according to his spouse, he "could not live or work without it."

Over the years, Schiller and Goethe had developed a remarkably close literary relationship. They conversed and corresponded about all sorts of topics, inspired each other, and even collaborated on some works. However, when they first met, Schiller was convinced that they'd never develop a solid rapport. This encounter took place in September 1788. They'd both been invited to attend a party hosted by the Lengefeld family. Schiller was particularly excited about the gathering, because Goethe was also on the guest list. But as the event wore on, Schiller realized that Goethe was only interested in chatting about his recent travels in Italy. Schiller was disappointed at the lack of in-depth conversation. He described the lackluster encounter in a letter to his friend Christian Gottfried Körner, noting, "I doubt whether we shall ever approach very near each other." But six years later, the two men met again, this time to discuss Schiller's new journal, *The Hours*. Their conversation during the second meeting was far more animated. And, eventually, their bond was so tight that Goethe observed, "One [of us] really could not live without the other."

Since he was a good friend, Goethe was welcome to stop by Schiller's home for an impromptu visit, as he did in the rotten apple incident. However, surprise guests who were less familiar with Schiller weren't as likely to receive a warm welcome. Schiller hated interruptions, particularly when he was hard at work. Goethe observed, "On these occasions he could now and then be very impatient, and sometimes even rude." If a visitor arrived unexpectedly, Schiller did not mask his frustration. His obvious annoyance would prompt a speedy end to the proceedings.

Schiller often wrote at night to ensure that no one descended on his doorstep while his pen flew. He'd work for hours while the stars were up and potential visitors were fast asleep. Schiller's body protested the night shift with inevitable drowsiness, but pangs of fatigue were no match for the writer. He sipped on strong coffee throughout the night to stay awake. Sometimes, if he was extremely tired, more extreme action was necessary. On these occasions, Schiller would plunge his feet into a tub of cold water to avoid falling asleep at his desk.

Schiller's neighbors may have been surprised to hear

that he had trouble staying awake at night. In 1797, he purchased a house on the western outskirts of Jena, Germany. During the summer months, he worked in a two-story tower in the garden of this home. His study was on the second floor of the square building. Late at night, neighbors would hear Schiller exclaiming loudly, as he paced back and forth, pondering his next line. This animated writing process lasted until some point between 3 a.m. and 5 a.m.

Schiller didn't always work at night. When he did pick up his pen during the day, it was in a darkened room. The red curtains in his study would remain closed. Sunlight illuminated the room through the lens of the fabric, providing a low-lit setting in which to work. Schiller was a master at molding his surroundings to fit his creative needs. The curtains, the apples, and the cups of coffee were props for the playwright's workday. And, as the red curtains rose and fell in his study, a variety of productions unfolded on the page.

In his youth, rather than mold his surroundings, Schiller had escaped them, all in the name of his grand literary ambition. His first play, *The Robbers*, opened when he was just twenty-two years old. Schiller had recently graduated from university and landed a job as an army medic in Stuttgart. At this stage in his life, for Schiller, the play trumped his military responsibilities. It was an exciting achievement for a young writer. Fully aware that he was breaking the rules,

Schiller snuck away to attend the first performance in Mannheim. If he'd simply returned to his duties, Schiller might have avoided trouble. However, he went to see another showing of the play, this time without any secrecy. Duke Karl Eugen doled out two punishments to the young rebel upon his return to Stuttgart. Schiller was locked up for fourteen days and, far worse, forbidden to publish anything other than medical papers.

Schiller was understandably reluctant to follow the duke's restrictive order. In order to ensure his literary freedom, he fled to Mannheim with a friend and coconspirator, Andreas Streicher. But even during these urgent proceedings, Schiller's creative whims took precedence over everything else. On the day they were to leave, Schiller was inspired to draft an ode. So he sat down and composed a new poem, despite Streicher's concern about increasing danger during the delay. Schiller's poetic detour set them back several hours. Though they'd planned to leave in the morning, the pair didn't set off in a wagon until late at night. Luckily they made it safely to Mannheim.

Schiller's escape was ultimately more difficult than he'd anticipated. He had trouble selling new work and was plagued by financial difficulties for many years. However, despite hardships, he did not deviate from the literary profession. Over the course of his career, he wrote major plays, including *William Tell*; poems, including "Ode to Joy"; and historical and philosophical papers. Schiller developed a methodology with the same verve and dedication that helped him produce these great works. The tall, skinny writer thus basked beneath dimmed light, sipped his caffeinated beverage, inhaled the smell of rotten fruit, and wrote.

The Nightlife

Like Friedrich Schiller, other great writers chose to write at night, but for a variety of reasons. For some, the wheels of creativity spun fastest after the sun set. "Night-time awakens a more alert chemistry in me," observed Tom Wolfe. He wrote *The Electric Kool-Aid Acid Test* late at night. Every afternoon, he'd start his workday, writing as many pages as he could before pausing for dinner. After dinner, Wolfe continued to write until he reached his daily quota of ten pages. Rather than drifting off to sleep as soon as he was done, Wolfe would round off his evening doing sit-ups in front of the television.

Robert Frost was also driven by creative forces to write at night, despite a deep-rooted fear of the dark. This phobia haunted Frost throughout his life. It drove him to sleep in his mother's room as a teen. Years later, in adulthood, Frost was not above asking someone to turn on the lights before he set foot inside his home. And yet, despite his trepidation, he chose to write at night. He found the nocturnal hours enchanting. Once, during an interview, he noted, "I always wished we had two moons. To see 'em weaving in the sky, it'd be quite a sky." As a novice farmer in Derry, New Hampshire, Frost established a radical work schedule. He composed his poetry in the evening, while the stars twinkled above the farmhouse. Then, rather than jumping out of bed to tend to the livestock at dawn, he slept until late morning. The cows did their part, adjusting to milking sessions at noon and midnight.

Other writers worked late because day jobs or school demanded their attention while the sun was up. Fyodor Dostoyevsky found time to write at night while he attended engineering school. He'd sit at his desk, huddled beneath a blanket, writing page after page of prose, while other students slumbered in their rooms. Even after he became a full-time writer, Dostoyevsky continued to write at night. The late hours provided a necessary calm, particularly as his fame grew. Just months before his death in 1881, Dostoyevsky mentioned his nocturnal habits in a letter. During the daytime, Dostoyevsky was distracted by numerous requests. He wrote, "Why do I write at night? But here I'll wake up now at one in the afternoon; then visitor after visitor will arrive."

As a teen in military school, J. D. Salinger was determined to find time to write. *New Yorker* editor William Maxwell described the young author's efforts: "At night in bed, under the covers, with the aid of a flashlight, he began writing stories." Later, when Salinger had as much time as he wanted to write, his work hours spilled into the day. He would spend up to sixteen hours straight writing and revising in the concrete bunker behind his home in Cornish, New Hampshire. Salinger's friend Bertrand Yeaton was one of the few people admitted into the reclusive author's study. Yeaton noted, "On the wall of the studio, Jerry has a series of cup hooks to which he clips sheaves of notes." Other essential tools in the room were a typewriter and a ledger, which contained manuscript pages and notes.

At night, Franz Kafka wrote for long stretches. In September 1912, he composed his short story "The Judgment" in one great gust, from 10 p.m. until 6 a.m. The next day, he wrote in his diary: "Only *in this way* can writing be done, only with such coherence, with such a complete opening of the body and the soul." A job at the Worker's Accident Insurance Institute prevented Kafka from writing during the day. He would sleepily report to the institute at 8 a.m., after writing for hours at night. Though Kafka finished work in the early afternoon, the remainder of his day filled up with lunch, a long nap, exercises (done while nude), a walk, and dinner. It wasn't until around 10 p.m. that he finally had a chance to write. Then, while the moon was high in the sky, his pen flew.

Joan Didion juggled a job at *Vogue* with her debut novel, *Run River*. When she got home from the magazine's office, Didion would look at her walls. They were covered in scenes from the book. She'd select a scene that hadn't been worked

on for months and take another stab at it. This ritual continued for years, until she sold the half-finished book to a
publisher. At that point, she spent a couple of months away
from the office, racing to the end both day and night.

In rare cases, an author might land a job that enables
him or her to write *and* earn a living at the same time. Working all night in a boiler room may not sound very appealing.
But for William Faulkner, the job of night supervisor at a
power plant was a perfect fit. Rather than nodding off during his overnight stretches, he wrote. In just six weeks, he
finished *As I Lay Dying*. All of his hours on the job paid off
twofold, with a steady paycheck and an entire novel.

By the Cup

HONORÉ DE BALZAC
1799–1850

Coffee is a great power in my life; I have
observed its effects on an epic scale.

—Honoré de Balzac,
from "The Pleasures and Pains of Coffee"

Sixteen-year-old Honoré de Balzac placed another order with his concierge. He wanted more coffee, a substance that was forbidden at Pension Lepître. But rules were often broken at the all-boys' boarding school, particularly when a savvy worker was eager to earn extra money. Balzac bought the smuggled goods on credit, and his debt would eventually force him to confess the illegal activity to his furious parents. The rebellious student must have felt that it was worth the trouble. Coffee was not a passing interest. It would serve as his constant writing companion, propelling him forward during a work regimen that lasted from night to day, with little rest in between.

Balzac was twenty when he first attempted to become a professional writer. To his father's disappointment, he chose this unconventional path over a career in law. After a few years as a junior law clerk, Balzac had decided that the legal process was depressing. Furthermore, he did not want to be trapped in a dull routine. Despite their criticism, Balzac's parents were willing to support the aspiring writer. With a steady allowance, he was able to move into an attic apartment near Place de la Bastille. In this new space, without the demands of a day job, Balzac devoted his days entirely to writing. And, during this time, he continued to develop an appreciation for coffee. In fact, coffee was one of the few comforts he could offer a visitor. In October 1819, he wrote to his sister, Laure Surville, asking, "When will you come see me, warm yourself at my fire, drink my coffee, eat my scrambled eggs, for which you will have to bring a dish?"

Meanwhile, Balzac sprang into his new vocation with tremendous zeal. When he did put down his pen, he roamed the neighborhood in search of inspiration. In an autobiographical tale, he recalled, "Being as poorly dressed as the workers and paying no heed to decorum, I aroused no suspicions." In the story, he even followed pedestrians so that he could eavesdrop on their conversations. During these expeditions, the narrator Balzac felt like he was, albeit briefly, part of a different class. He described the experiences as "the dreams of a waking man."

Toward the end of his two-year spell (the time period his parents allotted for the endeavor), Balzac raced to meet a deadline. There were only a few months left for him to finish *Cromwell*, a tragedy composed in verse, and his reputation, at least on a small scale, depended on it. Balzac planned to read the work to his family and friends, finally proving his ability as a writer. So he wrote for long durations, well into the night. In September 1820, he wrote to Surville about these herculean efforts. The aspiring author explained his feelings about *Cromwell* in terms of a substance he knew intimately. He wrote, "I treat my poor tragedy like coffee-grounds. I calculate what I shall distill from it, to make myself independent." He clearly felt that *Cromwell* could launch him to success. Balzac did complete the work, but he received unanimously poor reviews from his listeners. Still, he did not allow one failure to discourage him. The determined author picked up his pen and, with a coffeepot nearby, continued to write.

Balzac's late-night work stints may have been borne out of the practical necessity of hitting a deadline. However, he decided to adopt this practice on a regular basis. Over the years, he developed a habit of going to bed in the evening and waking just a few hours later. His workday began while the stars were still twinkling. While others slept, his imagination sparked and his pen flew.

In the 1830s, Balzac often retreated from Paris to the small town of Saché. In this quiet environment, out of the hubbub of the big city, he could concentrate on his writing. He would stay in the château of Jean de Margonne (a friend who was also his mother's lover). During his visits, Balzac stuck to a strict routine, waking to an alarm at 2 a.m. after settling down to sleep at 10 p.m. He'd write until late in the afternoon, consuming only toast and coffee all day long. Then he would break from work for a few hours to eat dinner with his host and other guests at the château. Writing was always a priority for Balzac. It was far more important than social interaction and sleep. The hardworking author believed that "too much sleep dogs the mind and makes it sluggish." And to keep his mind active, he relied on his favorite beverage.

Balzac consumed up to fifty cups of coffee a day, and he wouldn't settle for a subpar brew. While in Saché, he would make a half-day journey just to purchase quality coffee beans. He preferred strong Turkish blends. Balzac even developed his own method of preparing a pot of coffee to ensure it had a powerful effect. He deduced that less water and a finer grind translated into a supremely strong beverage. When he felt that the effect of coffee was waning, Balzac upped his dose. And when he needed a quick fix, he chewed on raw beans. The consumption of coffee had negative side effects. Balzac admitted that it could make him "brusque, ill-tempered about nothing." Despite his moodiness, Balzac chose to stick with coffee. He relied on it to maintain his long work hours. He observed, "[Coffee] gives us the capacity to engage a little longer in the exercise of our intellects."

Cup by cup, Balzac drafted *The Human Comedy*, his epic collection of interlinked stories and novels. While he wrote, the stocky author donned an unusual costume: a monk's robe. The long white fabric was lined with silk and held in place with a matching cord. A black silk skullcap completed the outfit. According to Surville, he started wearing this type of hat in the apartment near Place de la Bastille. She added, "It was my mother who always made these caps for him."

An obsessive reviser, Balzac never ceased to tinker with his work. While in the midst of composing his novel *The Country Doctor*, Balzac sent a letter to Eveline Hańska, a long-time pen friend, who would eventually become his bride. The thirty-three-year-old author wrote, "I am in the paroxysm of composition and can only speak well of it. When it is done you will receive the despairs of a man who sees only its faults." Balzac did not treat proofs as near-finished products. Instead, they were preliminary drafts, subject to numerous revisions. Balzac's short story "Pierrette" underwent seventeen rounds of proofs.

After Balzac turned a handwritten first draft over to a printer, the prose was typeset on large pages with wide margins so that he could input copious changes. His manuscripts tended to grow rather than shrink with each round, with additions far outweighing deletions. Balzac's changes would sprawl across each page. The marked-up proofs frustrated and confused his typesetters. In these days, when revisions meant resetting type, the task of inputting Balzac's changes was remarkably painstaking and laborious. In fact, there was a standing rule at Balzac's printer that workers spend no more than an hour on his proofs.

Balzac devoted his life almost completely to writing. He spent more time than most authors at his desk, with his pen soaring across the page. The result of his endless commitment was a large body of work. As he wrote to Surville in June 1833, "One can put a great deal of black upon white in twelve hours." And there was always a restorative cup of coffee nearby to help fire Balzac's synapses. The elixir was essential for Balzac to maintain his relentless schedule. Even his writing tools struggled to keep up with such ferocious dedication. In the same letter to Surville, he declared, "The poor pen! it ought to be made of diamond, not to wear out at this rate!"

Drinks with Inks

Whether they chose to fill their cups with tea or coffee, many famous authors have found that a nice hot brew is an ideal complement to the writing process. For Honoré de Balzac, coffee was a mental stimulant. However, he didn't reserve his coffee intake to the study. Balzac enjoyed sipping cups of fine coffee at Paris's historic café Le Procope. Voltaire, who died just over twenty years before Balzac was born, also frequented the café.

Voltaire's coffee consumption rivals Balzac's high intake. He was known to drink up to forty cups of coffee in a day. Le Procope was an ideal spot for the coffee enthusiast. Voltaire began frequenting the establishment in his early eighties. At the time, he was directing his play *Irène* in a theater across the street. After rehearsal, Voltaire would walk over to the café, sit down at his favorite table, and drink cup after cup of a special coffee-chocolate blend.

Benjamin Franklin was another famous literary patron

of Le Procope. He arrived in France in 1776, around the same time Voltaire had become a fixture in the café. Le Procope was one of Franklin's favorite spots to sit, drink, and converse. When Franklin died, Parisians mourned. As a signal of the widespread grief, the café was covered in black material for three days.

Jonathan Swift also enjoyed sipping delicious coffee. It seems that Swift liked to keep a healthy stock of his favorite beverage at home. His account ledgers show that he paid 1.2 shillings for seven pounds of coffee beans. In a letter to Hester Vanhomrigh, whom he nicknamed Vanessa, Swift advised, "The best maxim I know in life is to drink your coffee when you can, and when you cannot, to be easy without it." Though it is widely accepted that Swift was an avid coffee drinker, many scholars believe that he was using the caffeinated beverage as a code for sexual encounters in his letters to Vanessa.

Alexander Pope had a completely different use for coffee. He'd call upon a servant to whip up a pot of coffee in the middle of the night. Pope's late-night demand was for medicinal purposes. He found that the wafting steam from a fresh cup of coffee worked wonders for his recurring headaches. In addition to coffee, Pope was known to ring for ink and paper when a nocturnal muse struck. Pope's off-hour requests didn't go over well with servants. He developed a reputation for being a difficult visitor.

Other writers opted for tea over coffee. Simone de Beauvoir eased into her day with a cup of tea. In an interview for the *Paris Review*, de Beauvoir acknowledged that she wasn't much of a morning person. She observed, "In general I dislike starting the day." A dose of tea helped her make the transition from her bed to her desk. After consuming a cup of the hot beverage, she was ready to get to work (usually at around 10 a.m.).

C. S. Lewis once said to his friend Walter Hooper, "You can't get a cup of tea large enough or a book long enough to suit me." For Lewis, tea was a perfect literary companion. He preferred to drink tea alone, while he read or wrote. After working for a few hours in the morning, Lewis looked forward to a cup of tea landing on his desk. In his autobiography, he wrote, "If a good cup of tea or coffee could be brought to me around eleven, so much the better."

Samuel Johnson took his tea at all hours of the day. He was a fierce advocate of the substance. At one point, Johnson wielded his pen in defense of tea. The attack took shape in Jonas Hanway's "The Essay on Tea." Hanway argued against the consumption of tea in England. He even went as far to say that he would prefer to end "the custom of *sipping*." In his review of Hanway's treatise, Johnson detailed his own drinking habits. He described himself as "a hardened and shameless tea-drinker, who has for twenty years diluted his meals with only the infusion of this fascinating plant; whose kettle has scarcely time to cool; who with tea amuses the evening, with tea solaces the midnight, and with tea welcomes the morning." Johnson was clearly a devoted tea enthusiast, and he never did have to give up his favorite beverage.

Feeling Blue

ALEXANDRE DUMAS, PÈRE

1802–1870

Order is the key to all problems.

—Alexandre Dumas, père,
in *The Count of Monte Cristo*

Alexandre Dumas, père, walked out of another stationery store empty-handed. To his dismay, no one in Tbilisi carried the blue foolscap paper he desperately needed. He had traveled to Russia to attend a wedding in the summer of 1858. After the celebration, Dumas spent months exploring Eastern Europe, eventually landing in Tbilisi, the capital of Georgia. By this point he'd run out of his precious supply of blue paper. For decades Dumas had been using that particular color to pen all of his fiction. He was ultimately forced to settle for a cream stock, though he felt that color change negatively impacted his fiction.

The prolific writer had selected three colors as backdrops on which to compose. His poetry flowed on yellow, his articles unfolded on pink, and his novels hurtled on blue. Dumas worked at a startlingly rapid clip, and he was willing to bet on his ability to hit seemingly impossible deadlines. He once accepted a challenge to prove his speed by finishing the first volume of a novel, *The Knight of Maison-Rouge*, in just three days. Dumas won the wager, completing more than 3,375 lines several hours before the deadline. One secret behind his remarkable pace was to let the plot of a story simmer for a significant amount of time before he set pen to paper. He stated, "As a rule, I do not begin a book until it is finished." Thus, as he sprinted through a new novel, Dumas had a strong sense of the direction in which the tale was heading.

In 1844, Dumas struck it rich with two wildly popular newspaper serializations: *The Count of Monte Cristo* and *The Three Musketeers*. With his newfound wealth, he decided to have a mansion built in the small town of Port-Marly. After three years, the Château de Monte Cristo was complete. Dumas claimed not to have named the mansion, but rather adopted a name that a visitor bestowed upon it, when giving directions to her driver. The grand building was a celebration of the literary world, boasting a frieze of great minds from throughout history. Dumas, an extravagant entertainer, had the following statement inscribed in the entryway of the house: "I love those who love me." Within the grounds lived a remarkable assortment of pets, including peacocks, monkeys, dogs, cats, and a vulture.

Dumas's study stood off to the side of the main house. It was a two-story building, sparely furnished, with a study on the ground floor and a bedroom above. A small moat encircled the structure, emphasizing its role as a literary retreat or, if one went by its name, a form of prison. Dumas dubbed his little building Château d'If, after the formidable jail in *The Count of Monte Cristo*. The fictional spot was based on the real penitentiary with the same name, located in the Bay of Marseilles.

Rather than setting a regular appointment, Dumas squeezed in as much writing time as possible into each day. Soon after he woke, he had a pen in hand. He would dash off pages between errands and meals. Late at night, he could be found back in his study. It seems that his every spare moment was dedicated to writing. When he didn't have other obligations, or when a looming deadline forced him to focus on a particular project, Dumas worked up to sixteen hours a day. During these intense work periods, he had meals delivered to his study so he wouldn't have to break from writing.

Round-the-clock writing habits took their toll on the author. He suffered from intermittent fevers that lasted no more than a few days, but prevented him from picking up his pen. He would lie in bed, drinking only lemonade, until he recovered. At one point, Dumas developed insomnia and sought help from David Gruby, a Parisian doctor. Gruby came up with a peculiar regimen to help guide Dumas into a stable routine. He told his patient to get up early in the morning and purchase three apples. Gruby continued, "Eat the first at the Arc de Triomph [*sic*], the second at the Quai d'Orsay and the third at the Place de la Madelaine. Then return home on foot." Dumas was ordered to repeat the simple prescription on a daily basis.

Dumas's work regimen took a physical toll. However, this focus and dedication also helped pave the way to literary success. Over the course of his life, Dumas produced an impressive, almost baffling, quantity of work. In the span of ten years, he completed seventy volumes of novels, plays, and nonfiction books. His final tally of work exceeds three hundred volumes. Dumas was so prolific that some of his contemporaries questioned whether he had personally written everything credited to his name. In fact, Dumas did employ ghost writers to conduct historical research and outline plots. Of all Dumas's assistants, Auguste Jules Maquet is the most renowned. He collaborated with Dumas on several notable works, including *The Three Musketeers* and *The Count of Monte Cristo*. Their relationship, however, didn't last. Maquet was forced to sue Dumas for contractually owed payment. Dumas's use of ghost writers has prompted criticism over the years, but many people have remained staunch supporters of the author and his works. William Makepeace

Thackeray defended Dumas's methods, noting, "Does not the chief cook have aides under him?"

Thackeray's metaphor is particularly fitting in light of Dumas's following description of his writing process, which resembles a recipe. First, he lists his tools: "Paper (blue foolscap), pens, ink; a table neither too high nor too low." He continues with a straightforward list of steps: "Sit down—reflect for half an hour—write your title—then *chapitre premier.*" Then, he explains, it's a basic matter of calculating lines per page, pages per novel (two hundred for two volumes, four hundred for four volumes). It's unlikely the steps were this straightforward and efficient every time Dumas sat down to write. And he did note that much time was spent mentally planning his work before he put pen to paper. Nonetheless, he had, like a master literary chef, developed a methodology (and a color scheme) that worked well for him.

The Numbers Game

Alexandre Dumas, père, reportedly said, "My minutes are as precious as gold. When I put on my shoes, it costs me 500 francs." For Dumas, even a moment spent away from the desk meant significantly less output. He was an extremely fast writer, proved in his bet over the first act of *The Knight of Maison-Rouge* (see page 22). Over the course of his life, Dumas produced more than three hundred volumes of work. His stable of collaborators played an essential role in hitting that mark. Like Dumas, other famous writers soared through piles of pages every day. For some, the advent of the typewriter or, later, the computer allowed their fingers to race at even higher speeds.

Whether high or low, a daily word quota can be a source of pride for an author. William Golding announced at a party that he wrote three thousand words every day. Michael Foot questioned the claim, and a whiskey-fueled argument ensued. Norman Mailer sprinted into his career with three thousand words daily. Given Mailer's predilection for fighting, any skeptics would probably have hesitated to dispute the quantity. Arthur Conan Doyle also matched the daily output of these writers when he was at his most prolific.

Isaac Asimov typed a lightning-fast ninety, and sometimes one hundred, words per minute. At this speed, he produced up to four thousand words in just one day. Raymond Chandler didn't have a regular daily quota, but he could write up to five thousand words in one day. The quality of Chandler's prose was directly related to the speed at which it was produced. He stated, "The faster I write, the better my output. If I'm going slow, I'm in trouble. It means I'm pushing the words instead of being pulled by them."

Anthony Trollope was extremely disciplined. His workday began with a cup of coffee at 5:30 a.m. Then he worked for three hours, creating new material or rereading drafts. While he was writing, Trollope pushed himself to produce 250 words every fifteen minutes. He maintained this speed by keeping track of the time and his output with a watch.

Stephen King writes an impressive two thousand words per day, spending as much time as necessary to reach the quota. Similarly, Tom Wolfe would not stop writing until he reached his daily goal of eighteen hundred words. Though his daily word count wasn't as high as some other writers, Wolfe's pages really stacked up. Wolfe recalled that the first draft of his debut novel, *Look Homeward, Angel,* was four million words long. He noted, "I wrote the most of it standing up. I used the top of an old refrigerator for a table."

The daily quota for John Steinbeck and P. G. Wodehouse dwindled over time. At one point, Steinbeck wrote three thousand words a day, but that number tapered to two thousand. Wodehouse aimed for twenty-five hundred words daily when he started out, but settled into one thousand later in life. Graham Greene wrote five hundred words a day early in his career. Over time, he shifted to three hundred and then finally a mere one hundred words.

A handful of writers sit on the low end of the number spectrum. Once, after a full day of work, James Joyce proudly announced that he'd completed two sentences. Dorothy Parker revised so much that she wrote in a negative direction. She noted, "I can't write five words but that I change seven." James Thurber was a similarly obsessive reviser. He rewrote "The Train on Track Six" fifteen times. Of all the words that comprised his drafts, only one-twelfth made it into the final story. When asked if he envied faster writers, Thurber replied: "Oh, no, I don't, though I do admire their luck."

House Arrest

VICTOR HUGO
1802–1885

[He] entered his novel as if it were a prison.

—Adèle Hugo, on her husband composing
The Hunchback of Notre Dame

Victor Hugo's quill flew from one page to the next, and the stack of paper on his desk reached an unprecedented height. The twenty-eight-year-old author had been working on the same book from morning to night for months. He broke only to eat, sleep, and spend a precious hour with friends in the evening. These regimented visits didn't stray far from his book, as the entertainment often consisted of Hugo reading his latest pages. Hugo was a prisoner in his own home. It was a self-inflicted sentence to ensure that he finished *The Hunchback of Notre Dame* on time. The manuscript was due in a matter of months, and Hugo would incur a fine of 1,000 francs for every week it was late. His publisher had already extended his deadline twice and would not budge again.

Hugo was, at the time, living in a home in an otherwise uninhabited street near the Champs-Élysées. He'd moved there in the summer of 1830, after his previous lease was terminated. Apparently, there had been far too much activity, with visitors arriving day and night, for Hugo's landlady, who lived downstairs. In the fall, not long after he moved into his new residence, Hugo buckled down to work on the book. The deadline was February 1831.

Hugo procured a new bottle of ink in preparation for the marathon effort, but more extreme measures were necessary to enforce his confinement. He would have to forgo his cherished nightly strolls. This must have been a tremendous sacrifice. Hugo locked away his clothes to avoid any temptation of going outside and was left with nothing to wear except a large gray shawl. He had purchased the knitted outfit, which reached right down to his toes, just for the occasion. It served as his uniform for many months.

In September 1830, Hugo reported his progress in a letter to his friend, Victor Pavie. He wrote, "I am head over ears in *Notre-Dame*. I fill sheet after sheet, and the subject grows and lengthens before me to such an extent that I am not sure whether my manuscript will not reach the level of the towers." Hugo's isolation clearly sustained his productivity.

Though he had virtually locked himself indoors, Hugo

did not close himself off completely. He still maintained a small connection to the outer world through an open window. As the seasons turned, Hugo's window stayed propped open, even on cold winter days. In September he would have seen the leaves turn in the sparsely inhabited area where he lived. In early January 1831, when he was still working on the book, Hugo looked outside and caught an aurora borealis glittering in the night sky. A week later he finished the book, weeks ahead of the deadline. Hugo used an entire bottle of ink to write the book. Though he played with the idea of the apt title *What Came Out of a Bottle of Ink*, he settled on *Notre-Dame du Paris* (the American edition was renamed to highlight the hunchback character in the story).

When he wasn't under such a strict deadline, Hugo spent many evenings walking along Parisian streets, mentally drafting poetry, dialogue, and prose. He was a fearless pedestrian. Even after being pickpocketed near the Champs-Élysées, Hugo continued his nocturnal strolls. Three decades later, after leaving France, he still preferred to walk while he worked.

In 1855, Hugo moved to Guernsey, an island that, though just off the coast of France, is part of the British Isles. He'd been living in exile from his homeland since 1851, after Napoléon III came to power. Hugo bought an old mansion in his adopted country. He spent a great deal of effort on interior design. The rooms throughout the home were filled with elaborate and eccentric decorations.

Hugo's output was prolific during the fifteen years he spent in Guernsey. During this time he composed his epic novel *Les Misérables*, among other works. Hugo kept a steady routine in the grand home, which he called Hauteville House. He woke early every morning, washed his face with cold water, and then wrote for several hours. After writing, Hugo ate lunch and then devoted a couple of hours to exercise. One of his regimens consisted of an intense run followed by swimming naked in the ocean.

Hugo's study, which he dubbed "the lookout," was perched on the third floor of Hauteville House. With three walls of windows and a glass ceiling, the room had tremendous views of the surrounding landscape. A simple board attached to the wall served as a desk. When Hugo wanted to write, he lowered the board. It was positioned so that he could stand and face the ocean as he jotted down his work.

However, Hugo spent most of his time imagining his work away from the desk. Journalist Maurice Mauris visited Hugo in Guernsey and described the author's ambulatory process. He noted, "Even in his room he often walks up and down, like a caged lion, making occasional halts either before his desk to write the thoughts that have occurred to his mind, or before the windows, which are always open despite hot, cold, or rainy weather." Hugo was clearly creative while in motion. Whether inside or outside, he strode toward the next line of a story, a play, or a poem with each physical step.

Taking It in Stride

Throughout history, famous authors have ventured outdoors—into the wilderness or onto city streets. And, away from their studies and offices, they walked right into new ideas, which were later transcribed onto the page.

In his essay, "Walking Tours," Robert Louis Stevenson praised the virtues of a long walk. He found the practice altogether inspiring. He wrote, "This one, who walks fast, with a keen look in his eyes, is all concentrated in his own mind; he is up at his loom, weaving and weaving, to set the landscape to words." However, he clarified, "I do not approve of that leaping and running." In his opinion, one should fall into a steady clip during a walk. Stevenson felt that irregular speeds could be distracting. In August 1876, two years after the publication of this essay, the author embarked on a hike through the Cévennes Mountains in Southern France. He trekked more than 120 miles over the course of twelve days, with a stubborn donkey called Modestine as his sole companion. In terms of pace, rather than being in danger of leaping and running, one of his greatest challenges was simply maintaining a normal walking speed with the slow-moving donkey by his side. Stevenson's journey was captured in a memoir, *Travels with a Donkey in the Cévennes.*

Henry David Thoreau described walking as a noble art that few people had mastered. Thoreau found plenty of inspiration while on foot. He also admired William Wordsworth, who was an avid walker. According to Thoreau, Wordsworth's servant once directed a visitor to the poet's library but noted, "His study is out of doors." Thomas De Quincey estimated that Wordsworth walked around 180,000 miles in his lifetime. Though there's no map of Wordsworth's cumulative steps, his poetry offers literary markers for the epic trail. He composed many verses during lengthy jaunts in the countryside.

Robert Frost often retreated to the wilderness. He'd walk for hours alone in the dappled shade of trees. In college, Frost's classmates teased him about his habit of disappearing from campus. When they probed him about what he did during those solitary expeditions, he retorted, "I gnaw bark."

As a student at Oxford University, Aldous Huxley would walk for hours in the middle of the night. The nocturnal sojourns helped lift his spirits whenever he felt low. He observed, "Even if one wants to feel depressed one can't after an hour in the wind and the moonlight." Years later, he continued to walk. Huxley's daily routine was quite predictable. He divided his time neatly between writing and walking. Mornings were spent writing. Then, after lunch, he took off into the Hollywood Hills. Huxley would explore the Californian landscape for hours before returning home.

Charles Dickens was frequently compelled to walk. Pedestrians who spotted Dickens on the streets of London likely assumed he was late for an urgent appointment. Dickens moved at an impressive pace of 4.8 miles per hour. He would have zipped past leisurely strollers and brisk walkers alike. The author was propelled by a creative spark rather than the need to reach a physical destination. He embarked on epic walks while in the throes of composition. "If I couldn't walk fast and far, I should just explode and perish," Dickens wrote to his friend John Forster.

William Butler Yeats was frequently enveloped by gusts of creativity. The poet would barrel through city streets like a tornado. He'd wave his arms and mutter as he walked, so absorbed in musings that he lost track of the world around him. Swedish ambassador Erik Palmstierna, who was a friend of Yeats, spotted the poet on one of his outings in London. Yeats had unwittingly drawn a crowd with his wild composition. He only stopped after a gentle tap from Palmstierna.

Whether in the country or the city, Virginia Woolf enjoyed long walks. She often stumbled upon inspiration while out and about. Woolf found herself caught in a creative frenzy while strolling through London in late 1932. She recorded in her diary on November 2, "I have been in such a haze & dream & intoxication, declaiming phrases, seeing scenes, as I walk up Southampton Row." The story that gripped her in an imaginative fog would eventually develop into a novel called *The Years*.

As he did not know how to drive, poet Wallace Stevens walked to work. It was roughly two and a half miles from his doorstep to the offices of the Hartford Accident and Indemnity Company, where he served as vice president. During his commute, Stevens composed poetry. In an interview for the *New York Times*, he observed, "I write best when I can concentrate, and do that best while walking." Stevens recorded his poetry on slips of paper. Once he arrived at the office, he handed the slips to his secretary to be typed.

A Mysterious Tail

EDGAR ALLAN POE
1809–1849

For months I could not rid myself of the phantasm of the cat.

—Edgar Allan Poe, "The Black Cat"

In winter 1848, Edgar Allan Poe was swept up in a creative frenzy. He was working on an essay called "Eureka," which was an exploration of the "Material and Spiritual Universe." While Poe wrote, the household pet, a large tabby called Catterina, served as an affectionate literary guardian.

At this time, Poe was living in a small cottage in the Bronx. According to a visitor, who stopped by the quaint home in the fall of 1847, Catterina was always a fixture in Poe's work space. Sometimes Catterina crept onto his lap, but other times she chose a commanding spot to roost, right on his shoulder. There she watched Poe fill pages of prose with brown or black ink, "purring as if in complacent approval of the work proceeding under [her] supervision."

Catterina wasn't Poe's only writing companion. The author had lost his young wife, Virginia, the previous year. Virginia's mother, Maria Clemm, had lived with the couple for many years, and she remained with Poe after her daughter's death. Clemm was a kind, maternal presence in Poe's life. He often leaned on her for emotional support while in the throes of composition. Clemm observed, "He never liked to be alone." She would accompany Poe into their garden lined with fruit trees. As they strolled, Poe would talk enthusiastically about "Eureka," his evolving essay. At other times, charged by intense inspiration, Poe would spend hours at his desk. He worked tirelessly, throughout the night, until early morning. And, while he wrote, Clemm was there right by his side. She rested in a chair, letting her eyelids droop as the hours wore on. It seems that her presence was a great comfort to the writer.

Poe had lived with his two writing companions for a long time. Catterina pattered into the author's life in 1839. Poe was living in Philadelphia with Virginia and Clemm at the time. Biographer Hervey Allen described how Catterina, "in her burgeoning kittenhood, purred on the ample plateau of Mrs. Clemm's lap." The kitten quickly became an honorable member of Poe's family.

The narrator in Poe's story "The Black Cat" is haunted by a pet cat that he violently mistreated. Unlike his abusive character, Poe was a gentle, doting pet owner. And he developed a special bond with Catterina. Poe dutifully rolled out of bed to let her in or out in the middle of the night. When the author was away, Catterina missed him so much that she refused to eat.

In April 1844, Poe and Virginia had moved to New York. Clemm stayed behind with the cat, planning to move up later, once they had found a good place for all of them to live. After he arrived in the big city, Poe sent a letter back to his mother-in-law, writing, "Sissy [Virginia] had a hearty cry last night because you and Catterina weren't here." He also described the delicious feasts that awaited them day and night at their temporary boardinghouse. He added, "I wish Kate [the cat] could see it—she would faint." Unfortunately, with Poe's modest income, the entire family couldn't live in the fine boardinghouse. They found a cheaper option in the city and were reunited later that year. But by the winter, Virginia's health had declined and they decided to move to the Bronx.

Their small wooden home in the Bronx was surrounded by farms, and Poe had hoped that the fresh country air would help Virginia recover from tuberculosis. But he was a struggling author, with little money, and wasn't able to offer any luxuries for the ailing woman. Virginia slept on a simple straw bed, covered in an old overcoat that belonged to Poe. Catterina offered what help she could, in the form of body heat, by curling up on Virginia's chest. Mary Gove Nichols wrote about a visit to the home during this time: "The coat and the cat were the sufferer's only means of warmth, except as her husband held her hands, and her mother her feet." After Virginia died in August 1847, Poe stayed in the Bronx with Clemm and their cat. Though he grieved deeply, with Catterina on his shoulder and Clemm by his side, Poe still managed to write.

In the cottage, Poe worked beneath the sloping roof of his attic study or in the cozy living room. His handwriting was unusually neat. In fact, recipients who reviewed Poe's manuscripts often commented on the meticulous script. George Graham published many of Poe's pieces in his eponymous magazine. He described Poe as "wandering from publisher to publisher, with his fine, print-like manuscript, scrupulously clean and neatly rolled." Poe's final drafts were composed on separate pieces of paper which he then stuck together with sealing wax. With the end of one sheet attached to the beginning of the next one, the papers formed one long piece. The entire text was then wound into a tight scroll. When Poe recited his work, he'd produce one of the scrolls. He was always impeccably dressed, and most often elected to wear a completely black suit. Standing before his audience, in his signature attire, he would commence. And as the story or poem progressed, he'd let the scroll fall to the ground.

Scrolling

Like Edgar Allan Poe, Jack Kerouac was partial to scrolls. However, his process differed from Poe's post-writing assembly (see page 42). In 1951, Kerouac put *On the Road* down on paper in one great gust. He had been planning the book for some time and had plenty of notes from previous years in his journals.

He decided that an extremely long strip of paper would suit his project perfectly. So he taped pages together and, over the course of three weeks, typed his novel. The scroll allowed Kerouac to maintain a rapid clip without having to pause and reload his typewriter at the end of each page. When he was done, Kerouac triumphantly brought the lengthy tome to his editor, Robert Giroux at Harcourt, Brace. Giroux recalled, "[Kerouac] took one end of the roll and he flung it right across my office, right across the desk and stuff." To his dismay, Giroux focused on the unusual packaging. He asked, "But Jack, how can you make corrections on a manuscript like that?" Giroux recalled saying, "Jack, you know you have to cut this up. It has to be edited." Kerouac left the office in a rage. It took several years for Kerouac's agent, Sterling Lord, to finally find a home for the book, at the Viking Press.

The Traveling Desk

CHARLES DICKENS

1812–1870

Before I tasted bit or drop yesterday, I set out my writing-table with extreme taste and neatness, and improved the disposition of the furniture generally.

—Charles Dickens, in a letter to John Forster after arriving at a vacation spot in Broadstairs, Kent

In June 1846, a box addressed to Charles Dickens arrived in Lausanne, Switzerland. It contained an eclectic assortment of statuettes: two bronze, rotund toads, frozen at the end of a climactic sword fight; an eccentric dog salesman, surrounded by his pups, also in bronze; and a rabbit balanced on a leaf. In addition to the mini menagerie, there was a paper knife, a green vase, a desk calendar, blue ink, and writing quills. Dickens needed each one of these items, all in the right place, before he could set to work on his novel *Dombey and Son.*

Dickens was deeply attached to the objects that sat on his writing desk. His son described the ornaments as something "for his eyes to rest on in the intervals of actual writing." He found creative comfort in the familiar view. As soon as the precious package arrived, Dickens arranged the pieces on his desk. And, with the stage set, he was finally able to pen a tale about the Dombey family.

Wherever he stayed, whether home or away, Dickens adjusted the surroundings to fit his needs. He required that his study contain the same design in each locale, and his preferences went beyond the workroom. When he arrived in a new space, he would arrange everything, from furniture to luggage, before drifting off to sleep. Author Eliza Lynn Linton recalled that Dickens was even particular about the direction his bed faced: north to south. She recalled, "He backed up his objections by arguments about the earth currents and positive or negative electricity. It may have been a mere fantasy, but it was real enough to him."

Dickens insisted on order in his home, and it must have been difficult to maintain with ten children. On rare occasions he allowed disruptions in this private space (see page 78). Dickens's study was always immaculate, but his need for cleanliness permeated the entire home. The children's rooms were inspected by Dickens on a daily basis.

He kept a steady routine, writing from 9 a.m. to 2 p.m.

every day, during which time he expected complete quiet. He preferred to use blue ink, though his choice was not based on color preference. Rather, a special blue ink dried much faster than other colors, which meant he could skip the bothersome task of blotting his work. In the afternoons, Dickens went for a walk, which was never a stroll. His pace was remarkably fast (see page 37).

As much as Dickens preferred to travel with his study, there were times when he simply needed to get away. When *The Pickwick Papers* first appeared, Dickens was out of London. So he decided that, for luck, he would be out of town for other first publication dates. If a friend dropped by his house to congratulate him on a new work that had just come out, it was likely Dickens was far from the city, hoping for good fortune to hit once again.

Quilled Muses

Charles Dickens was wild about birds. He owned a talking raven named Grip. Dickens was very fond of the mischievous bird, which often exclaimed "Halloa, old girl" and "I am a devil." The pet served as the model for a loquacious raven of the same name in Dickens's *Barnaby Rudge*. Edgar Allan Poe believed that Dickens could have made better use of the talking bird. When Poe reviewed *Barnaby Rudge*, he argued, "[Grip's] croaking might have been prophetically heard in the course of the drama." This criticism has led many scholars to believe that Grip was the inspiration for Poe's best-known poem, "The Raven."

Flannery O'Connor was also inspired by birds, though of a completely different feather. As a child she had a chicken that could walk backward, a talent that landed them in a cinema newsreel clip. O'Connor owned a variety of birds: chickens, pheasants, ducks, turkeys, and quail, to name a few. But peacocks were her true passion. In her mid-twenties

O'Connor mail-ordered six peacocks, a peahen, and four peachicks, and they captivated her immediately. Eventually an ostentation of forty peafowl strutted around her farm, Andalusia. The striking creatures also popped up in her fiction and were the focus of an essay, "The King of Birds."

In his autobiography, William Butler Yeats wrote about George Moore's extreme affection for a blackbird. Every morning the bird would perch in the garden across the street from the Dublin-based author's apartment and serenade him. Moore kept his windows open so that he could enjoy the blackbird's songs while he wrote. At some point, Moore began to worry about the safety of his winged friend. Moore's neighbor owned a cat, for whom the blackbird would make a tasty meal. The concerned author at first threw stones at the cat, but then he went one step further and built a trap for the troublesome feline. Moore's neighbor reported his eccentric acts against the cat to the local Prevention of Cruelty to Animals organization. And, Moore reported to Yeats, rather than trapping the cat, he accidentally trapped the bird. Though Yeats believed most of Moore's story, of the trap part, he wrote, "The rest of the tale fills me with doubt."

Birds aren't necessarily friendly. An aggressive seagull can terrify its human target. Daphne du Maurier was walking to a farm in Cornwall, and along the way, she saw a farmer plowing a field. A flock of hungry seagulls assembled above the man, swooping around him while he worked. The scene inspired du Maurier's short story "The Birds" (the film version of the story, set in California rather than Cornwall, was directed by Alfred Hitchcock).

Paper Topography

EDITH WHARTON
1862–1937

True originality consists not in a new manner but in a new vision. That new, that personal, vision is attained only by looking long enough at the object represented to make it the writer's own.

—Edith Wharton, from *The Writing of Fiction*

Edith Wharton's dream home was a mansion seated on top of a hill in Lenox, Massachusetts. She had overseen the creation of the estate from conception to final touches. From 1903 to 1911, Wharton lived in this grand building, which she considered her "first real home." Wharton often invited guests to visit, including elite literary friends, like author Henry James. A guest at her home would not have needed to rush in the morning. There were views to admire from the mansion, aptly named the Mount. The impressive home presided over an artfully designed garden, with colorful flower beds and impeccably manicured hedges and lawns. Laurel Lake glittered in the east and the Berkshire hills faded into the distance. Breakfast would have been delivered to the visitor's room. And if he or she had any questions or concerns, a maid could be summoned with the simple press of a button. James described the Mount as a place where "comfort prevails." Meanwhile, during these early hours, the hostess was tucked away in the most private room on the second floor—and she was undoubtedly still in bed.

Wharton spent her mornings beneath a rose-colored bedcover, but she wasn't squandering her time with extra sleep: She was writing. Wharton's friend Gaillard Lapsley was among the select few who were admitted into the author's room during these precious early hours. He recalled Wharton sitting up in her silk nightgown and matching cap, with "the dog of the moment under her left elbow and the bed strewn with correspondence, newspapers and books." Wharton used a writing board, which rested against her knees. She kept an inkpot by her side, even though, in its position, it was liable to fall at any moment. There she sat, in the comfort of her bed, composing stories about the high society milieu to which she belonged.

Wharton put a great deal of effort into the floor plan of the Mount. Interior design had been her passion since childhood, and so naturally she took great interest in the development of her house. In fact, before she turned to fiction, Wharton cowrote *The Decoration of Houses* with Ogden Codman Jr. Wharton selected the most isolated, quiet spot on the second floor for her bedroom. Her husband, Teddy, slept in an adjoining room and very rarely spent the night with his wife. Apparently sharing the bed triggered Wharton's asthma. The marriage was also troubled from the outset. And when Teddy became mentally ill, it dissolved completely. Wharton's bed at the Mount was not a site for companionship. It was a place where she could work peacefully and comfortably alone.

In *The Writing of Fiction*, Wharton observed, "The impression produced by a landscape, a street or a house should always, to the novelist, be an event in the history of the soul." It seems fitting then that, in a reflexive act, Wharton molded her fictional landscapes into paper topographies. She wrote in blue ink on pale blue stationery, thoroughly revising her prose until it was difficult to read. At that point, she'd rewrite sections on strips of paper and glue them over the illegible parts. Or she would cut up the original page and arrange the slips on another piece. The rise and fall of strips on each page marked the evolution of her prose.

When Wharton completed a page, she let it drop to the ground. Later in the day, a maid would whisk into the room to pick up the scattered paper. Then Anna Bahlmann, Wharton's secretary, would type the handwritten prose.

However, even the typed manuscript was subject to change. Wharton polished her prose, round after round, until she felt it was ready to send to a publisher.

Bahlmann did not begin working with Wharton as a secretary. She had originally served as twelve-year-old Wharton's governess in New York City. The young Wharton was an enthusiastic student, who gravitated to all sorts of literature. As a child, Wharton had already begun to pen her own stories. She composed her work on blank brown pieces of wrapping paper that had been salvaged by the household maids.

Apparently Wharton's family wasn't enthusiastic about her literary aspirations. The author wrote about their negative reaction to her writing in her autobiography, *A Backward Glance.* And yet several biographers have observed Wharton's tendency to mythologize her life story. In one instance, Wharton stated that she was forbidden to read fiction. However, her claim is contradicted by the fact that Wharton's family members, including her father, gave her novels as gifts. It does seem that there was at least a degree of resistance against Wharton's writing in her home. She vividly recalled showing a short story to her mother, Lucretia. In the opening scene of the story, a character refers to her messy drawing room. Lucretia offered no praise in response. She simply stated, "Drawing rooms are always tidy." Wharton's mother may not have approved of literary ambition, but in Bahlmann the young writer found a true advocate.

When Wharton married Teddy in 1885, Bahlmann came with her. She served as secretary in the new household, transcribing Wharton's prose along with other duties. In May 1890, Wharton dashed off an enthusiastic letter to Bahlmann. She wrote, "A few days ago I sent to Scribner's a little story—my first attempt at publishing prose—& to my surprise it has been accepted. Isn't this a delightful beginning?" The story, "Mrs. Manstey's View," marked the start of Wharton's career as a fiction writer (she had successfully sold poems in the past). Bahlmann stuck with Wharton throughout her career, helping type a number of works, including *The House of Mirth* and *Ethan Frome.* She stayed with Wharton in many different homes around the world, from New York and Massachusetts to London and France. Their working relationship ended two decades after Bahlmann first took on the role of secretary. At that juncture, Bahlmann's declining health prevented her from continuing. Three more women served as Wharton's literary secretaries: Dolly Herbert (briefly), Jeanne Duprat, and Jeanne Friderích.

Wharton contended that originality was "attained only by looking long enough at the object represented to make it the writer's own." That long look for Wharton was not a passive act. She developed her own method to reshape the object in her view. Nestled in the comfort of a bed, Wharton constructed her prose—writing, rewriting, cutting, pasting—and building a world of fiction along the way.

Bright-Eyed

Many great writers, like Edith Wharton, composed their masterpieces as the sun was rising. Ray Bradbury stated, "I start [writing] whenever my subconscious gives a helluva yell and tells me to get out of the way." Though he was subject to creative whims, Bradbury still made sure that he sat down to work by 9 a.m. every morning.

Famous authors who worked early in the morning or late at night (see pages 7 and 61) tend to share one thing in common. Philip Roth recalled an observation from Joyce Carol Oates about authors and their work schedules. Oates noted that when writers ask one another about their regimens, they really want to know, "Is he as crazy as I am?" Roth added, "I don't need that question answered." But an offbeat schedule isn't necessarily a crazy choice. Many authors need to wrap themselves up in their work, and the best time to do this is when most other people are sleeping. These authors can concentrate more fully during off-hours, without those myriad of distractions that storm into one's life during the day.

For some writers, mornings are the only practical time to write. As a young mother, Toni Morrison wrote before her children woke up. "Writing before dawn began as a necessity," she noted. But later, when she was no longer restricted to certain hours by a day job or her parental duties, Morrison found that mornings still suited her best. "I'm not very bright or very witty or very inventive after the sun goes down," she observed.

For Morrison, an essential element of her writing process is witnessing the evolution of night into day. Every morning, before she writes, she drinks a cup of coffee while watching the sun rise. She observed, "I realized that for me this ritual comprises my preparation to enter a space that I can only call nonsecular."

Katherine Anne Porter also preferred to compose in the morning, particularly because it was such a peaceful time. While discussing her early work hours, Porter noted, "I don't want to speak to anybody or see anybody. Perfect silence."

For Wallace Stegner, it was essential to divide his days between a morning of writing and everything else in the afternoon. By allocating a full morning to writing, Stegner had enough time to let his fiction balloon into a reality. He wrote, "I know no way to become convinced, and stay convinced, of the reality and worthiness of a novel but to go out every morning to the place where writing is done, and put your seat on the seat of the chair."

For one reason or another, many authors have found creative solace in the morning. From early birds to late risers, here's a roundup of when these writers punched in to work:

4:00 a.m.: Sylvia Plath

5:00 a.m.: Jack London, Toni Morrison, Katherine Anne Porter

5:30 a.m.: Anthony Trollope, Kurt Vonnegut

6:00 a.m.: W. H. Auden, Graham Greene, Ernest Hemingway, Victor Hugo, Vladimir Nabokov, Edith Wharton

7:00 a.m.: Johann Wolfgang von Goethe

8:00 a.m.: Flannery O'Connor, Wallace Stegner

9:00 a.m.: Ray Bradbury, C. S. Lewis, Thomas Mann, Gabriel García Márquez, Leo Tolstoy, Gore Vidal, Virginia Woolf

9:30 a.m.: Carson McCullers

10:00 a.m.: W. Somerset Maugham

The Cork Shield

MARCEL PROUST
1871–1922

I never knew how many hours he slept, or even if he slept at all. It was all between him and the four walls of his room.

—Céleste Albaret, Marcel Proust's housekeeper

In September 1914, Marcel Proust told his housekeeper, Céleste Albaret, that they would not be embarking on another vacation. They had just returned to Paris after spending time in Cabourg, a resort town on France's northern coast. The author spoke of his literary efforts in light of World War I, which had recently begun. "The soldiers do their duty, and since I can't fight as they do, my duty is to write my book, do my work. I haven't the time for anything else," he declared. Albaret observed that this was a turning point, "when he deliberately entered into his life as a partial recluse." *Partial* is a key word in Albaret's description. Though Proust is often depicted as a writer who never left his home, he did go out on occasion. However, he did choose more often than not to isolate himself in his bedroom. He wrote at night and slept during the day, hours that reinforced his seclusion from the rest of the world.

In Search of Lost Time (originally translated as *Remembrance of Things Past*) is the multivolume novel that Proust felt obligated to write. He'd begun working on the first installment, *Swann's Way*, in 1909, and it was finally published in 1913. Even at this point, Proust had developed a reputation of being a literary hermit. In an interview that took place not long after the publication of the first book, he described the creative benefits of his reclusive lifestyle. He said, "Darkness, silence, and solitude, by throwing their heavy cloaks over my shoulders, have forced me to recreate all the light, all the music and the joys of nature and society in myself."

The space into which Proust retreated was located on the bustling Boulevard Haussmann in Paris. He lived on the second floor of number 102 from 1906 until 1918. Proust had moved into the apartment after his beloved mother's death. He couldn't bear to continue living in the same place where both his parents died. The apartment had belonged to Proust's uncle. The family connection appealed to the sentimental author. However, it couldn't have been worse for Proust's health and work routine. Proust had suffered a severe asthma attack when he was nine years old. Because of his condition, he tried to avoid dust and pollen, which were prevalent on the tree-lined street.

During the day, pedestrians strode and strolled outside Proust's window. Automobiles sputtered and carriages clattered over the cobblestone road. All the commotion kicked up noise and dust, which filtered into the apartment building. After many sleepless days, he managed to convert his room into a cocoon, one that would keep out sound, light, and pollutants. Shutters, double-pane windows, and large blue silk curtains all served as layers to protect Proust from irritants entering his bedroom. In fact, they were closed throughout the apartment. Proust only allowed Albaret to open the windows when he was out. Proust even decided to get rid of his telephone to ensure greater solitude. In this sealed-in space, there were no stray rays of light or extra specks of dust to bother the slumbering writer during the day.

Noise, however, was an entirely different matter. Proust was plagued by the sounds that charged into his room. His friend Anna de Noailles offered him a practical, albeit unusual, solution: cork! She had lined her own bedroom walls in cork to help dampen outside noise, and found that it worked well. So he followed her advice. In 1910, he had his bedroom walls and ceiling covered in sheets of cork. However, he didn't have the panels covered in wallpaper, as de Noailles had, and the layer of cork turned black over time.

Occasionally Proust went out to visit friends or eat dinner at the Hôtel Ritz, but he spent most nights nestled in his bedroom. Around the room sat a collection of writing tools and resources and family memorabilia, which ranged from his mother's grand piano and cabinets to photographs and smaller items. His bed was tucked in the corner. Proust would lie back on the mattress, with layers of sweaters wrapped around his shoulders, and write. Stocks of pens, ink, and notebooks were stored on the three tables by his side. Proust used simple wooden pens with interchangeable metal nibs. His pages rested on his knees and were illuminated by the low glow from a bedside lamp (a chandelier overhead was rarely used). And, from night to morning, while the busy city rested, Proust's pen whirred across the page.

Albaret described this nighttime regimen, the hours of which she also adopted, as an "upside-down life." She lived in Proust's home for a decade, following his schedule, keeping the apartment in order. She delivered croissants, prepared fresh coffee (never letting him drink a cold cup), tidied the scattered pages on his bed, and tended to his every need.

Proust would write, rewrite, and rewrite again. Every time he reread his work, he thought of something to change or add. He explained to Albaret, "I want my work to be a sort of cathedral in literature. That is why it is never finished. Even when the construction is completed there is always some decoration to add, or a stain-glass window or a capital or another chapel to be opened up, with a little statue in the corner." Always meticulous with details, he would sometimes embark on research trips to study particular people or things up close. The smallest nuances, such as the construction of a garment or the posture of an acquaintance, were of great significance to Proust. Consequently, he was constantly adding new material to his expansive novel. Revisions spilled down the margins of his drafts. When he ran out of room, a piece of paper marked with new text was pasted onto the manuscript. Albaret had come up with this clever process in order to ensure that the changes were input correctly.

In 1919, Proust was suddenly forced to move out of his treasured apartment on Boulevard Haussmann. His aunt, who owned the building, sold it without informing her nephew first. According to Albaret, Proust had the cork lining removed from his bedroom and placed in storage, presumably to be used again down the line. However, other biographers note that the sheets were sold to a bottle cork facility.

Proust found a new apartment at 44 rue Hamelin in Paris. He lived there, on the fifth floor, for the final years of his life. Unfortunately, Proust passed away before he could correct the final three volumes of *In Search of Lost Time*, but they were published posthumously. The entire tome was more than three thousand pages long. It was the product of thousands of nights of work. Alberet observed, "The miracle with M. Proust was his will power. And his will power was all directed towards his work."

Flea Circus

COLETTE

1873–1954

Shall I ever marvel enough at animals?

—Colette, from her novel *Break of Day*

In 1926, Sidonie-Gabrielle Colette bought a vacation home in Saint-Tropez, an idyllic town on the French Riviera. She spent many summers at La Treille Muscate, the name of which was inspired by an old muscat grapevine in the garden. Colette's friend the painter André Dunoyer de Segonzac also had a home in Saint-Tropez. He often visited La Treille Muscate. While he was there, he observed Colette as she prepared for work. He later described a strange habit that would often precede Colette's writing.

Colette would study the fur of her French bulldog, Souci, with a discerning eye. Then she'd pluck a flea from Souci's back and would continue the hunt until she was ready to write. Dunoyer de Segonzac described this grooming ritual as a method of procrastination. Like a reluctant swimmer, Colette performed little tasks before diving into the papers on her desk. In addition to relieving Souci of her fleas, Colette would cozy up with a pug on the divan. She would also swat a number of flies. Only then was the author ready to sit down to work.

The shift from stalling to writing was always abrupt, according to Dunoyer de Segonzac. Colette would suddenly be moved to write. Then she would plant herself at a desk that faced the corner of her room. There she sat for hours at a time. Though the pages flew, Colette moved very little while she wrote. Inevitably, she grew cold. Her third husband, Maurice Goudeket, recalled, "She put rug after rug on her knees and shawl after shawl on her back." After particularly long periods of writing, Colette looked "like a cocoon" with all of her layers.

In an article for the *New York Times*, Diane Ackerman observed of Colette's flea-picking habit, "It's not hard to imagine how the methodical stroking and probing into fur might have focused such a voluptuary's mind." Ackerman wrote that Colette practiced the prewriting treatment on her cats (there's no mention of the dogs). Certainly, in Saint-Tropez there were plenty of cats to groom. Colette had ten feline pets, not counting the strays that came to visit. In fact, cats and dogs had been curling up by her side since childhood.

Colette's mother, Sido, adored animals. On occasion Sido even brought a hunting dog to church, much to the chagrin of the local priest. Colette grew up in a manor in Saint-Sauveur-en-Puisaye, Burgundy. Under Sido's watch, generations of cats and dogs were born in their home. Litters of kittens and pups played and snoozed in their downstairs living room. And when Colette walked to school, the family's bulldog, Toutouque, trotted along beside her.

At twenty Colette married Henry Gauthier-Villars, and he whisked her off to Paris. Gauthier-Villars, better known by his pen name, Henry Willy, was far from an ideal husband. He was an unabashed cheat, who went as far as bringing women home, even when Colette was there. Willy also exploited unknown authors, paying them unfairly small sums to ghostwrite his books. He was always on the lookout for new material to bring in more money. He was not above adding his wife to the roster of ghostwriters. He asked Colette to write a novelization of her experiences as a schoolgirl. She complied, filling up several exercise books, but Willy rejected the novel after a cursory glance.

However, a couple of years later, after a second read, Willy changed his mind. He asked Colette to incorporate a few scandalous relationships into the story, and she reluctantly obeyed. Then he sold the novel, *Claudine at School*, to a publisher under his name. Colette was merely known as the inspiration for the book. *Claudine at School* was a hit, and Willy urged Colette to pen more books starring the same protagonist. To ensure the pages mounted, Willy routinely locked his wife inside a room to write for four-hour stretches.

Colette felt trapped in her awful marriage. She was lonely and depressed. Two of her most steadfast companions during this difficult time were a dog and a cat. Colette wrote, "I had a [French] bulldog, Toby-Chien, who lived in a turmoil or a swoon of emotion, and a long, luxurious, subtle angora cat, Kiki-la-Doucette." When Colette traveled to a country house, where she lived alone for the second part of each year, Toby and Kiki came with her. And when her marriage finally fell apart and she moved into a new apartment, thirty-one-year-old Colette brought the animals along. "It was there that I faced the first hours of a new life, between my dog and my cat," she recalled.

Bit by bit, Colette established herself as an independent woman. She found success as an actress, had affairs with men and women, and began to sell fiction and nonfiction under her own name, first as Colette Willy and then simply as Colette. *Gigi*, published in 1944, was her most famous novel.

Animals were always close to Colette, whether they were at her heels or on her lap, and both on and off the page. Cats and dogs served as protagonists in many of her stories. In Colette's *The Cat*, a man's affection for his kitty creates a rift in his marriage. The story may have resounded with Henry de Jouvenel, Colette's second husband. De Jouvenel felt like he was intruding when he stumbled upon his wife when she was alone with her pets. He proclaimed, "One of these days you'll retire to a jungle." Colette tossed the idea up in the air, like a mischievous kitten with a ball of yarn. She wrote, "I keep toying with the agreeable picture of the future this prophecy offers me."

Paws
Between the Pages

Colette is one of many famous writers who not only adored but were also inspired by their pets. In the canine realm, John Steinbeck wrote about driving around the country with his poodle in *Travels with Charley*. Elizabeth Barrett Browning wrote a poem about her cocker spaniel called "To Flush, My Dog." She described her relationship with Flush in a letter to a friend, writing, "He & I are inseparable companions, and I have vowed him my perpetual society in exchange for his devotion." Viriginia Woolf also wrote a novel, *Flush*, about the poetess and her dog.

During the evening, Emily Brontë often sat and read beside Keeper, the family dog. Keeper was a large, ferocious-looking animal. When incited, he would erupt in loud, deep barks. He was an intimidating dog, but Brontë was not afraid of him. In one instance, when Keeper brawled with another dog, she broke up the fight. Her secret weapon in this instance was pepper, which she tossed onto both dogs' noses. According to Ellen Nussey, a biographer and friend of the family, Brontë's treatment of Keeper was sometimes abusive. Nussey recalled that, to punish the dog, Brontë once hit his eyes repeatedly until they were swollen. And yet, Nussey observed, "She never showed regard to any human creature; all her love was reserved for animals."

William Styron found inspiration on walks with his dog, Aquinnah, in Roxbury, Connecticut. At home, Styron was plagued by trivial matters. But out in the woods, with his loyal companion, he was able to ponder his writing. He observed, "Without a daily walk and the transactions it stimulates in my head, I would face that first page of cold blank paper with pitiful anxiety."

Feline muses abound in the literary world. In a humorous letter to his three-year-old grandson, T. S. Eliot wrote: "I am glad you have a cat but I do not believe it is so remarkable a cat as My cat. . . ." The cat he was referring to was a pet named Jellylorum. This kitty was immortalized in Eliot's collection of feline poems, *Old Possum's Book of Practical Cats*. She's also a character in the musical *Cats*, which was based on Eliot's book.

Edgar Allan Poe had a pet cat that inspired him to write an essay, "Instinct vs. Reason—A Black Cat," which appeared in January 1840 in *Alexander's Weekly Messenger*. In this piece, Poe described the antics of his dexterous feline, who would routinely perform a singular trick. She would leap from the floor and secure her paw below the latch on the kitchen door. She had to get the sequence just right: unlocking the latch, pushing it down, and then springing away with enough force for the door to fly open. If she fell, the determined cat jumped up and tried again until she'd completed her mission. Poe's admiration of the spry feline is evident as he introduces her to the reader, noting, "The writer of this article is the owner of one of the most remarkable black cats in the world—and this is saying much; for it will be remembered that black cats are all of them witches." According to scholar Thomas Ollive Mabbott, the black cat preceded Catterina, a tabby that would perch on Poe's shoulder as he wrote (see page 39).

In the 1930s, Ernest Hemingway lived in Key West, and dozens of polydactyl cats wandered around the grounds of his home. However, he found his favorite feline companion the following decade, when he lived in Cuba. Around sixty cats lived on Hemingway's Cuban estate, and there was one in particular who rarely ever left his side. It was a black-and-white cat named Boise. He trotted alongside Hemingway on his strolls and kept him company while he worked. Boise, along with a few of the author's other cats, appears as a character in his posthumously published novel *Islands in the Stream*.

Like Boise, many household pets curled up by their owners while they wrote. Raymond Chandler had a black Persian cat named Taki, who kept him company in his workroom for almost twenty years. Chandler called her his secretary. Taki had a habit of plunking down on whichever papers he needed at the time. She was also one of Chandler's toughest critics. In a letter to Charles Morton, an editor at the *Atlantic Monthly*, Chandler wrote that Taki spent time "just quietly gazing out of the window from a corner of the desk as if to say, 'The stuff you're doing is a waste of time, bud.'"

Though he was reluctant to share his study with a troop of kittens, Charles Dickens had little say in the matter. His cat, Williamina, was determined to care for her newborn kittens in that room. Dickens, on the other hand, was determined not to be disturbed. Twice the kittens were transported out of the study. On the third attempt, Williamina carried each precious kitten in through a window, back into her chosen room. At this point, Dickens gave up, and found a way to work amid the purring, climbing, and playing. He even kept one of the kittens. This kitty, who was simply called "the Master's cat," extinguished a candle twice with his paw while Dickens was reading. It was a clever ploy to divert the author's attention away from work so they could play, and it worked.

Traffic Jamming

GERTRUDE STEIN
1874–1946

I saw her once, perched high up on the front seat with Alice Toklas beside her, driving down the avenue des Champs-Elysées in this strange vehicle, very distinguished among the rush of quite different, lesser cars, paying no attention to the jokes and laughs of the crowd.

—Art historian Daniel-Henry Kahnweiler,
on Gertrude Stein

Gertrude Stein obtained her first car in 1917. She quickly discovered that the driver's seat of a Model T Ford was an ideal spot to write. In the privacy of an automobile, she could let her mind wander and jot down a few lines, no matter where she was. Stein was especially productive during errands. She'd sit in the car while her partner, Alice B. Toklas, dashed into a store. While she waited, Stein would pull out a pencil and a scrap of paper. She was particularly inspired by the traffic on busy Parisian streets. Automobiles stopped and started with a rhythm that thrummed right into her poetry and prose.

Stein's *Autobiography of Alice B. Toklas* details their lives through Toklas's perspective. In this book, "pictures and automobiles" are described as Stein's only "two real distractions." Stein's love of cars sprung from her volunteer efforts during World War I. Toklas came up with the idea to volunteer while they were walking in Paris. She had spotted a woman driving a car for the American Fund for French Wounded (AFFW) and decided it was the right organization for them. The AFFW was comprised of American women who transported a variety of supplies to hospitals. A car was necessary for traveling around the country. So, before they could begin, Stein and Toklas had to produce a vehicle. Before this time, Stein had never owned—or driven—a car.

Members of Stein's family in the United States helped raise funds for the car. Meanwhile, Stein learned how to drive (Toklas preferred to ride along in the passenger seat). Stein's friend, William Cook, was an artist earning a living as a taxi driver. Cook helped teach her the basics, though she was never confident reversing the car. Instead, she simply found ways to power forward, terrifying passengers and other motorists in the process. Her friend William Rogers recalled, "She regarded a corner as something to cut, and another car as something to pass, and she could scare the daylights out of all concerned."

Stein's car, the Model T Ford, was shipped all the way from America. It arrived in France in February 1917. The automobile was humorously dubbed Auntie, after Stein's Aunt Pauline, who "always behaved admirably in emergencies and behaved fairly well most of the time if she was properly flattered" (*The Autobiography of Alice B. Toklas*). At times Stein found it difficult to flatter the stubborn car. After being forced, again and again, to wind up the unreliable engine, she made empty threats to scrap poor Auntie.

Stein and Toklas drove around France, making rounds to wherever they were needed, sometimes on perilous, snow-covered roads. Stein was not fond of using a map, though her instinct wasn't always reliable. So they often followed a long, unpredictable route to reach their destination. AFFW members were forced to maintain and fix their own cars, but Stein only conducted minor repairs herself. She was always able to wangle help whenever she needed to do anything more complicated than changing a spark plug.

During their travels, Stein and Toklas dined at homes and restaurants all over the country. The most delicious dishes they ate are recounted in Toklas's *The Alice B. Toklas Cookbook*. Between meeting soldiers, braving country roads, and trying new cuisine, Stein squeezed in time to write, often while seated in Auntie.

After the war, Stein and Toklas were forced to get rid of their dear car. While dining at a restaurant in the Bois de Boulogne, Toklas had been pulled aside by a police officer and informed that trucks were no longer allowed on the roads in the park now the war was over. "So would Madame see that her truck did not appear there again," he instructed. Meanwhile, after all of that driving around the country, Auntie was only capable of making short trips. Eventually, the car simply stopped working for good, right in the middle of a city street.

A new car was needed, one that fit within Stein and Toklas's budget. They ordered another Ford, and to save money, they selected a version that lacked most amenities, such as a cigarette lighter and a clock. When it arrived, Toklas observed that the car, with its bare dashboard, "was nude." Stein promptly pronounced, "Godiva." And so their new car was named after a woman who, legend tells, rode horseback naked to protest unfair taxes.

Stein kept up her habit of writing in the driver's seat of the new car. And even when she wasn't in Godiva, mere proximity to cars could spark her imagination. Stein preferred to keep watch over mechanics while they worked on her cars. On a winter day, while she waited for Godiva to be fixed, Stein settled onto the steps of a nearby dilapidated Ford. From that vantage point, she could guard her precious automobile and write at the same time. By the time the car was ready, Stein had finished an entire essay called "Composition as Explanation."

There is also a possibility that a car mechanic was involved when Stein first heard the term "lost generation," which Hemingway later made famous, using it in an epigram for his novel *The Sun Also Rises*. According to Stein, she was discussing the younger generation who had served in World War I with a hotel owner, and he said that they were "a lost generation." However, in two versions of this story, Hemingway placed the historic conversation in a car garage. While Stein didn't mention a mechanic in her account, her friend Bravig Imbs was at the hotel and he wrote that she also spent a long time talking to a young mechanic there.

On the Move

Gertrude Stein isn't the only the author who found inspiration en route from one destination or another. From the outset of a journey to the point of arrival, there's a chunk of time that, for many writers, is full of potential. Those hours or minutes don't have to be spent snoozing or pondering a crossword puzzle. Great works have been scribbled into notepads on cars, trains, and planes. Stein and Vladimir Nabokov (see page 121) both spent time writing in the solitude of their parked cars. When he was a struggling writer, Raymond Carver would also hole up in his car in order to work in peace. However, his first wife, Maryann, pointed out that Carver wasn't quite as misfortunate as people believed. She noted that whenever they could afford it, he would always rent out a room somewhere just to write.

Some famous writers composed their novels on the move, whether it was in a vehicle or riding an animal. A car can function as a stationary room, perfect for writing. However, it would be a difficult feat for authors to write while driving. Eudora Welty managed to jot down ideas on the long drive to visit her mother in a nursing home. Somehow she managed to steer and write at the same time (see page 145).

Sir Walter Scott composed the lines to his poem *Marmion* on horseback. Rather than pulling over to contemplate the lines, he preferred to write in motion. Much of the piece was written while riding his horse through the hills surrounding the village of Lasswade, near Edinburgh, Scottland. He recalled his writing process during a ride in the same area with his son-in-law, John Gibson Lockhart. Scott said, "Oh, man, I had many a grand gallop among these braes when I was thinking of 'Marmion.'"

However, most writers who composed on the move weren't in the driver's seat (or on an animal). As a passenger in a train or a plane, one doesn't need to pull over to record an idea. And there isn't the necessity of directing the reins while mentally drafting lines, like Scott. In his late twenties, John le Carré took full advantage of a ninety-minute commute from Buckinghamshire to London. He was working as an M15 officer at England's foreign office. During his train ride, le Carré penned his debut novel, *Call for the Dead* (published in 1961). He also squeezed in time to write during his lunch hour. Le Carré directed most of his energy to writing. "I was always very careful to give my country second-best," he later quipped. Trains are now far more efficient than they were in the 1950s and '60s, which means commuters do not have to spend as much time traveling. However, increased efficiency isn't necessarily a good thing. Le Carré observed, "The line has since been electrified, which is a great loss to literature."

Joseph Heller stumbled upon some great ideas while riding the bus. In fact, he noted, "The closing line for *Catch-22* came to me on a bus." For Heller, the bus ride, like other mundane activities during the day, allowed him time to think alone. He put all of his ideas down on index cards and referred to them while working on a novel.

Sixteen-year-old comedian Woody Allen managed to write during his subway ride to an after-school job at an advertising agency in New York. Unlike le Carré, Allen didn't have the luxury of a seat. He recalled, "Straphanging, I'd take out a pencil and by the time I'd gotten out I'd have written forty or fifty jokes . . . fifty jokes a day for years." So, even while standing, he managed to produce an impressive output during each ride.

Elie Wiesel has written just about anywhere. In an interview for the *Paris Review*, he listed off a few places where he was able to write: "On a plane, in a café, while waiting." After World War II, he spent many years reporting for French and Israeli publications. Wiesel credited his experience in journalism for the flexibility to write in all sorts of places.

Margaret Atwood has found inspiration while soaring above the clouds. When she was asked by the *Guardian* to offer some commandments about the art of writing, composing on planes was at the top of her list. She advised, "Take a pencil to write with on aeroplanes. Pens leak. But if the pencil breaks, you can't sharpen it on the plane, because you can't take knives with you. Therefore: take two pencils."

Tunneling
by the Thousands

JACK LONDON
1876–1916

*Well, well, plenty of dig, and an equal amount of
luck may enable me some day to make perhaps
a small livelihood out of the pen.*

—Jack London, in a letter to Mabel Applegarth

When twenty-one-year-old Jack London first attempted to
launch his career, he toiled for fifteen hours every day. He
lived with his family in San Francisco at the time. The work
was mentally and physically exhausting. Food came second
to work, and London's prose grew in direct opposition to his
growling stomach. He transcribed stories and articles from
longhand with a borrowed typewriter and developed blis-
ters from pounding on the exasperatingly resistant keys.

London's back and shoulders ached from the intensive regimen. He threw himself entirely into the task. Unfortunately, despite his fierce perseverance, the young writer failed at his first attempt to make a living as an author. After receiving a flurry of rejection letters, he was forced to find paying work. London took a menial job in the laundry room at a boys' preparatory school. He suffered for a few months amid dirty clothes and steam. Then, in July 1897, London took off north to the Klondike in search of gold.

While in the North, London trekked through the treacherous wilderness. He followed the same path as many other ambitious and adventurous Americans. But only a select few struck it rich during the Klondike gold rush. London returned home virtually empty-handed. Still, the twenty-two-year-old had a glint of determination in his blue eyes. He decided to spin his perilous adventures into literary riches. London believed that he could tunnel his way to publication with sheer will and hard work. "Dig is a wonderful thing, and will move more mountains than faith ever dreamed of," he proclaimed. So, upon his return, London dug toward his dream, furiously and tirelessly, like the most determined miners in the Klondike.

Again, London took a seat at his desk. He wrote line after line, racing toward one fixed goal. He had decided to become a professional author, and there was no obstacle great enough to stop him. As he moved from one page to the next, London drew closer to his dream. The aspiring author broke from writing and researching only to sleep. His bedroom lamp glowed until 2 a.m., and he sprung back to action at the sound of his alarm clock at 5 a.m.

London took great care to learn the art of writing. Each sentence he penned was a study in form. London spent hour upon hour analyzing work by successful contemporary writers. He wanted to follow in the footsteps of literary giants. And, in fact, there were times when he traced the same path as his favorite author, right on the page. London was an avid fan of Rudyard Kipling. He decided that the best way to master Kipling's prose was to copy it word for word. It was an arduous task, but London didn't mind hard work, particularly if it might lead to success. He later acknowledged, "I would never have possibly written anywhere near the way I did had Kipling never been."

London developed a writing maxim based on the need not simply to write, but to make a living as a writer. His stepfather had passed away while he was in the Klondike, and a large share of family responsibility fell to him. So he established a strict rule of writing at least one thousand words per day, hoping that the prolific output would lead to a steady career.

Sometimes it seemed to London that he might never break into the publishing world. Though he rarely wavered from his goal, he did experience serious bouts of despair. At one point, London even considered suicide. The weight of 650 rejection letters bore down on the poor, struggling author. However, his depression abruptly disappeared when he finally received an acceptance letter. *Black Cat* magazine made the first financially solid offer for one of his stories, and it saved London, as he observed, "literally, and literarily."

After his career took off, London continued to write a thousand words daily, whether on land or the high seas. On a yacht in the Pacific Ocean he still managed to fit in two hours of writing every morning. And on his ranch in California, London kept a steady morning work regimen. He woke promptly at 5 a.m. but didn't go very far: He liked to work in bed. Note cards were fastened to a string above his head, lingering until they were processed and replaced with fresh ones. Below those frozen thought bubbles, London wrote steadily until he reached that same quota he had established as a young writer.

London planned each story carefully before transcribing it onto the page. "Have at least learned to compose first, to the very conclusion, before touching pen to paper," he wrote to his longtime friend Cloudesley Johns. This method involved few revisions, which enabled London to barrel forward. Yoshimatsu Nakata, London's servant, recalled that the author used "a blunt fountain pen with a wire tube at the end—a stylograph." A regular fountain pen would have slowed London down; with this tool he didn't have to worry about the way the nib faced. With London's remarkable dedication to high-volume productivity, it's no wonder he completed more than fifty books in his brief lifetime.

London was described as the "Kipling of the Klondike." The accolade serves as a fitting end point for the struggling author who sat copying out his hero's prose. And, to add to the glory, Kipling himself became a fan of London's work. Scooping through the pages with a tireless hand, London proved his declarations about hard work as a twenty-something. All of that digging clearly worked!

In the Shadow
of Masters

Many great writers developed their voices, in part, by tracing the words of their favorite predecessors. While Jack London handwrote Rudyard Kipling's stories, Ray Bradbury hammered out pieces by authors he admired on a typewriter to help perfect his own prose. In moments of utmost despair, Bradbury dropped entire paragraphs by Tom Wolfe into his drafts. "Because I couldn't do it, you see. I was so frustrated!" he proclaimed in an interview for the *Paris Review*. As a teen, Joan Didion learned to type while copying out Ernest Hemingway's work. She was particularly impressed by his "perfect sentences."

Rewriting a favorite novel is one way to absorb the style of a literary master. Other writers chose to read a particular book every day before they set to work. The process of reading helped each of these authors warm up before setting pen to paper. French author Stendhal read a government text every day before composing his novel *The Charterhouse of Parma*. In a letter to Honoré de Balzac, Stendhal wrote,

"In order to acquire the correct tone I read every morning two or three pages of the Civil Code." Somerset Maugham developed a ritual of reading Voltaire's *Candide* before diving into a new novel. "So that I may have in the back of my mind the touchstone of that lucidity, grace and wit," he noted.

Willa Cather read the Bible before she wrote. According to Thornton Wilder, Cather wanted "to get in touch with fine prose." He noted that she regretted choosing an archaic text, but the habit had already stuck. Maya Angelou also found inspiration in the Bible, which she kept nearby when she worked. When asked why she used the Bible, Angelou responded, "For melody. For content also. I'm working at trying to be a Christian and that's serious business."

A Writer's Easel

VIRGINIA WOOLF

1882–1941

She took her hand and raised her brush. For a moment it stayed trembling in a painful but exciting ecstasy in the air. Where to begin?

—Virginia Woolf, from *To the Lighthouse*

Virginia Woolf, in her twenties, wrote every morning for two and a half hours. Her desk was three and a half feet tall, with a top that could be angled up so she could view her work up close or at a distance. According to her nephew Quentin Bell, Woolf stood at this desk so that her sister, Vanessa, would not outdo her. Vanessa was an artist who painted while standing. Bell observed, "This led Virginia to feel that her own pursuit might appear less arduous than that of her sister unless she set matters on a footing of equality." Though she may have developed the habit out of sibling rivalry, she stuck with it. For years, the tall, striking author arrived at her literary easel and wrote.

In 1917 Woolf and her husband, Leonard, founded a small publishing house called Hogarth Press. Woolf was deeply involved with the fledgling company, but she did not give up writing. Every morning, promptly at 9 a.m., Woolf strode past the printing press, which sat in the front room of their basement. She walked straight into the storage room, which was also her writing space. The room was located just beyond the center of operations of the little publishing company, at the back of the house.

By this time, Woolf had transitioned from standing to sitting while she worked. Every morning she would settle into a cozy old armchair, with her writing materials in hand. She used a piece of thin plywood as a writing surface. Hogarth Press was also Woolf's publisher, which meant that her manuscripts made an exceptionally short journey from point of origin to print. The finished product landed right back in the storage room, shelved alongside books and galleys by other writers, before it was sent out to readers and reviewers.

Years later, Woolf was still using a writing board. In a diary entry from January 1933, she wrote, "I am so delighted with my own ingenuity." A simple alteration promised to significantly improve her writing process. She had attached a tray for pens and ink to her writing board. Virginia was thrilled at the prospect of having plenty of writing materials nearby. That way, she would no longer risk losing a flash of inspiration in the brief time it took to get up and find the appropriate tools.

Meanwhile, Woolf's admiration of her sister's visual talent did not diminish over time. Vanessa's paintings were used for Woolf's book covers and, sometimes, interiors. In a letter to her sister, Woolf praised her execution of the cover for *Kew Gardens*. She wrote, "I think the book will be a great success—owing to you; and my vision comes out much as I had it."

Woolf, in her own way, painted her own pages of prose. Rather than settling for standard black ink, she filled her pens with purples, greens, and blues. Purple, her favorite color ink, can be found in letters, diary entries, manuscript drafts, and page proofs. When Woolf was twenty-five, she had a book printed in purple ink and bound in the same color leather. The novel, *Friendship's Gallery*, was a gift for her friend Violet Dickinson. Woolf's love letters to Vita Sackville-West were also in purple. Most of *Mrs. Dalloway*, her most famous work, was composed in purple, too. In October 1938, Woolf wrote in her diary about the sky, which, like so many of her pages, had been painted in a purple hue. She wrote, "A violent storm—purple ink clouds—dissolving like blots of ink in water."

Board Writing

Roald Dahl, like Virginia Woolf, used a writing board while sitting in an armchair. Dahl's neighbor Claud Taylor handcrafted the board, repurposing billiard-table material for a soft surface. With a Dixon Ticonderoga pencil in hand and a yellow legal pad on the green board, Dahl was ready to write.

Robert Frost sat in a chair with a large board resting on the arms. The board was propped up by a smaller one, so that it sat at a slight incline. Apparently just about any surface *except* a table would work for Frost. In an interview for the *Paris Review*, he proclaimed, "I use all sorts of things. Write on the sole of my shoe."

The Full Spectrum

It's not surprising that many great writers, like Virginia Woolf, were very particular about the ink they used. Though ideas spark in the mind, the right tools can facilitate a writer's creativity. Lewis Carroll shared two quirks with Woolf. He preferred to compose his work while standing at a tall desk and he used purple ink. The color choice, for Carroll, had been made for him, and not for literary purposes. He taught mathematics at Christ Church College in Oxford. Beginning in 1870, the teachers were expected to use purple ink on their students' work. Carroll began using the color to pen his fiction, too.

Langston Hughes wrote many letters to Alice Walker. And, she noted, "to my delight he always used bright-green ink!" Rudyard Kipling wrote, "For my ink I demand the blackest, and had I been in my Father's house, as I once was, would have kept an ink-boy to grind me Indian-ink." He could not stand any variation in the color of his ink. It had to be dark black.

In one case, an author attempted to use several colors in the spectrum. William Faulkner knew that the Benjy sections in *The Sound and the Fury* were difficult to follow. So when he met his editor at a speakeasy in New York, Faulkner proposed a solution: They could use a colored ink! A variety of colors would represent the different time periods in Benjy's narrative. The costs, however, would have been astronomical, and the idea was quickly dismissed. Faulkner lamented, "I wish publishing was advanced enough to use colored ink." Bennett Cerf planned a limited color edition of the book, but it was never published. In 2012, eighty-three years after *The Sound and the Fury* was first published, Faulkner's wish was finally granted. The Folio Society released a special edition with fourteen different colors of ink.

Crayon, Scissors, and Paste

JAMES JOYCE

1882–1941

It is a genuine example of the art of mosaic. I have seen the drafts.

—Valery Larbaud, on Joyce's *Ulysses*

James Joyce lived in Trieste from his mid-twenties to his early thirties. When he was twenty-nine, he recruited his sister Eileen to move from Dublin and help watch over his two young children. Eileen recalled Joyce's unique habits during her time with him. At night, he would often retreat to bed, though not to sleep. The Irish native would lie on his stomach, armed with a large blue pencil, and write. The most peculiar detail, however, was his nocturnal uniform. Before he began, Joyce donned a white coat. At first glance, this may have seemed like pure eccentricity, but it was a practical choice. Eileen noted, "He always wrote with a white coat on—it gave a kind of white light." Joyce's sight was failing. His coat served as a beacon amid blurry surroundings, presumably reflecting extra light onto the paper. The resourceful author established these habits while composing his debut novel, *A Portrait of the Artist as a Young Man.*

Joyce's eye problems began in childhood with myopia. But it wasn't until his twenties that his sight took a severe downward turn. When he was twenty-five, Joyce developed rheumatic fever and, along with it, a painful eye disease called iritis. As the years progressed, he was afflicted with a slew of illnesses that affected his eyes, including glaucoma, cataracts, and conjunctivitis. In 1917, Joyce underwent his first eye surgery. By 1930, there had been twenty-four more operations, and none restored his sight.

Joyce struggled to read and write with poor vision, and was often nearly completely blind. French critic Louis Gillet wrote, "I still see him, in order to decipher a text, placing the paper sideways and bringing it into the narrow angle where a ray of his ruined sight still subsisted." Joyce forged his way with innovative tools, like the white coat, and sheer determination. He described epic work sessions on *Ulysses* to his patron, Harriet Shaw Weaver: "I write and revise and correct with one or two eyes about twelve hours a day I should say, stopping for intervals of five minutes or so when I can't see any more."

A typewriter might have lightened Joyce's workload, but he flatly rejected the idea. The machine would have inevitably sped up his writing, and he preferred to compose slowly and meticulously. Joyce's close friend Frank Budgen recalled discussing typewriters with the author in Zurich. Budgen had observed that Joyce was far less prolific than some of his peers. Joyce countered, "But how do they do it? They talk them into a typewriter. I feel quite capable of doing that if I wanted to do it. But what's the use? It isn't worth doing." He had been toiling on *Ulysses* line by line, word by word. After a productive day Joyce reported to Budgen that he had completed two sentences. He explained, "What I am seeking is the perfect order of words in the sentence." Joyce was committed to writing at his own pace and in his own hand, directly on the page, which led to an increasingly difficult predicament as his sight worsened.

One of Joyce's greatest obstacles was frustratingly simple and nearly impossible to overcome: He needed to see the writing on the page. As Joyce's sight deteriorated, the thick lenses in his glasses were not strong enough for the task. He used two pairs of glasses and a magnifying glass to review page proofs of *Ulysses*. Three magnifying glasses were necessary for *Finnegans Wake* proofs.

In fact, to compose this final book, Joyce magnified the

entire production. His most notoriously complex novel unfolded in giant script. In a letter, Joyce informed Weaver that he finished a passage of *Finnegans Wake* on a large piece of paper with a charcoal pencil that often broke. He added, "I have now covered various large sheets in a handwriting resembling that of the late Napoléon Bonaparte when irritated by reverses." It seems that crayons were more resilient tools. Padraic Colum, a fellow Irish author, recalled, "The actual writing of the text was done by Joyce on long strips of paper—sometimes cardboard—with different colored crayons." Joyce used a variety of colors to compose and revise the work, from red and orange to green and blue.

Despite the physical stress of writing, Joyce obsessively revised his work, well into final proof stages, frustrating his printers to no end. He was equally compulsive when it came to jotting down ideas, rarely missing an opportunity to snatch up something that he might later slip into the text. While working on *Ulysses*, Joyce kept pieces of paper in his waistcoat pocket. "At intervals, alone or in conversation, seated or walking, one of those tablets was produced, and a word or two scribbled on it at lightning speed," recalled Budgen. Joyce found endless amusement in the world around him. He accumulated a broad array of information, from scientific and historic facts to foreign-language puns. He kept the notes in orange envelopes, transferring them later into notebooks or onto sheets of paper.

It was impossible for Joyce to single-handedly conduct the extensive research in Paris needed for *Finnegans Wake*. His sight was too poor to scour books and publications for words and facts. But he was not afraid to delegate. Joyce's wife, Nora, remarked, "If God Almighty came down to earth, you'd have a job for him." He recruited amanuenses and research assistants, many of whom were family and friends. Colum, who was one of his charges, recalled, "He did not want any of us to brief him, for example, on astronomy or finance. But the name of a star or a term in finance— 'sterling,' say—would give him what he needed."

Joyce was, in his words, "a scissors and paste man." He snipped words and phrases from his surroundings— whether it meant delving into a book or simply observing the world around him—and he distributed them into *Ulysses* and *Finnegans Wake*. Joyce's notebooks stored these concepts, and he used colored pencils and crayons to keep track of what was transferred into manuscripts. Valery Larbaud wrote about Joyce's *Ulysses* notebooks: "It makes one think of the boxes of little coloured cubes of the mosaic workers."

Joyce had no standard approach. A color might represent a section of a book on one notebook page, and elsewhere, it might indicate the date it was transferred. Joyce's notebook pages are thus stunning and elusive, a medley of color impossible to precisely unravel or trace.

Though his sight paled, Joyce blazed a bright and colorful path—with crayons, pencils, and charcoal—into print. And whether it meant a special coat or sprawling handwriting, the determined author found every way he could to see the page.

Cigarettes, Twins, and the Evil Eye

SUPERSTITION AT THE WRITER'S DESK

After four years of working on *Finnegans Wake*, James Joyce was exhausted, and it dawned on him that another writer could finish his book. "It would be a great load off my mind," he confessed to Harriet Shaw Weaver. And he had found an ideal candidate: a Dubliner named James Stephens. He approached Stephens with this idea, and the latter agreed to step in, but only if necessary.

Joyce approved of Stephens's work, but he also liked that they shared the same first name. Additionally, Stephens was one letter away from Stephen, Joyce's protagonist in *A Portrait of the Artist as a Young Man*. Another binding detail turned out to be false, but Joyce nonetheless believed it at the time. Joyce was under the impression that he and Stephens were born in the same hospital on February 2, 1882. Joyce's superstitions seemed to have influenced his choice. Even Stephens pondered the issue: "Joyce loved me. Or did he? Or did he only love his birthday, and was I mere coincident to that?"

Joyce got as far as planning a byline for the coauthored book: It would be JJ & S (also, Joyce pointed out, an acronym for John Jameson and Son's, the whiskey distillery). However, Joyce ended up laboring through the book to its end. Meanwhile, he remained good friends with his delegated twin.

Many famous authors, like Joyce, followed superstitions with great zeal. Somerset Maugham had an ancient Moorish symbol inscribed onto the gatepost of his villa in the French Riviera. The emblem represents the hand of Fatima warding off the evil eye. It appeared throughout his home, on the fireplace, on cigarette cases, and even on matchboxes. It was printed on the spine, cover, or interior of each of Maugham's books, beginning with his third novel, *The Hero*. Maugham picked up the symbol from his father, who stumbled upon it while traveling in Morocco. The writer used it for good luck and once reported to a visitor, "So far, it's worked."

Graham Greene had a peculiar obsession with numbers. When Greene visited Evelyn Waugh in the countryside, he would break from writing and spend long periods on the side of a road. Every now and then a car passed, and Greene would take note of the license plate number. In an interview for *Harper's Bazaar*, Waugh recalled, "He could not write another word until a certain combination of numbers—I think it was 987, something like that—appeared to him by accident."

In an interview for *McCall's*, Truman Capote confessed, "I used to be fantastically superstitious, I mean to the point of mania." Though he made up many of these superstitions, Capote found it difficult to abandon them. He wouldn't begin or end a piece of work on a Friday. He had an aversion to the number 13. He'd trade hotel rooms or avoid making a call if the number 13 was somehow involved. At one point, he would even jump on his thirteenth step. Capote never let the number of cigarette butts in an ashtray exceed three (extra ones were placed in his coat pocket). He also refused to board a plane with more than one nun.

A composer inspired Jack Kerouac's superstitious habit, though his Catholic background may have also played a part in the literary ceremony. In an interview for the *Paris Review*, the Beat writer recalled, "I had a ritual once of lighting a candle and writing by its light and blowing it out when I was done for the night . . . also kneeling and praying before starting (I got that from a French movie about George Frideric Handel)."

Isaac Asimov wasn't nervous about writer's block. "In twenty years," he proclaimed, "I haven't frozen at the typewriter." Asimov's fear, however, was that his writing tools would fail him. He kept two electric typewriters so that he could keep working if one broke.

Leafing Through
the Pages

D. H. LAWRENCE
1885–1930

I find a forest such a strange stimulus.

—D. H. Lawrence, about the Black Forest near
Ebersteinburg, Germany

In an obituary for D. H. Lawrence that appeared in the *New Yorker*, Janet Flanner claimed, "He had, among other eccentricities, a fancy for removing his clothes and climbing mulberry trees." It isn't clear how the reporter obtained this scandalous tidbit, and many people refuted the claim. Lawrence scholar H. T. Moore described Flanner's report as "ridiculous." Anaïs Nin dismissed the journalist's "sensational picture." It appears that Flanner's depiction of Lawrence was founded on unsubstantiated gossip. Yet there was at least one thread of truth in her claim: Lawrence was drawn to trees.

In fact, once after too much white wine, Lawrence decided to fetch mimosa blossoms for a couple of refined guests. The inebriated author fell from the branches, and the women were not amused. Typically, though, he was sober around trees. Lawrence spent many mornings leaning back against the trunk of a tree, with a pad of paper on his lap. And he found more than shade beneath the branches; trees were a source of inspiration.

"The trees are like living company," wrote Lawrence in a letter to painter Jan Juta. He was referring to the great firs that populated the Black Forest near Ebersteinburg, Germany. Thirty-five-year-old Lawrence spent a couple of months in the quaint German village. In this idyllic locale, he often retreated to the woods to work on *Aaron's Rod*, his seventh novel. The entire book was composed outside, where fir trees offered quiet companionship. Lawrence felt inextricably linked to the impressive forest that served as his outdoor work space. He observed, "[The trees] seem to give off something dynamic and secret, and anti human—or nonhuman."

Four years later, Lawrence sought refuge beneath pine trees in North America. At the time, he was living with his wife, Frieda, and their friend Dorothy Brett. Their home, Kiowa Ranch, was located on a mountain in rural New Mexico. Lawrence would disappear into the woods in the morning. Around noon Brett might look for him to announce lunch. She'd inevitably find him absorbed in his work beneath a tree. Brett wrote, "Sometimes one can glimpse you through the trees, sitting leaning up against the trunk of a pine tree, in your blue shirt, white corduroy pants, and big, pointed straw hat." If not deep in the woods, Lawrence could be found working on a bench beneath a massive pine that towered in front of the ranch.

Throughout his career Lawrence basked in the spotted shade of a variety of trees around the world. At Chapel Farm Cottage in Hermitage, England, he sat in a chair beneath an apple tree and wrote. Lawrence worked near lemon trees in Gargnano, Italy. There he reviewed proofs of *Sons and Lovers* and worked on several pieces of poetry and prose. In Mexico, he worked under the embrace of a willow tree by a lake. And he penned *Lady Chatterley's Lover* under a large umbrella-pine tree in Tuscany.

In 1926, Lawrence received a visit in Italy from friend and fellow writer Aldous Huxley. Huxley had just bought a new car and offered to sell his old one to Lawrence. The idea of driving did not appeal to Lawrence at all. In a letter recounting the incident, Lawrence declared, "It is much pleasanter to go quietly into the pine-woods and sit and do there what bit of work I do. Why rush from place to place!"

When in Doubt...

Sometimes the best way to revise is to rewrite. D. H. Lawrence rewrote entire books, starting fresh right from the beginning. He preferred to compose a completely new draft rather than tinker with the text of a previous version. *Lady Chatterley's Lover* was written three times before Lawrence settled on the final manuscript.

Like Lawrence, Jennifer Egan was brave enough to discard a full manuscript. Her first complete draft of a book was a six-hundred-page dud. Egan received no positive reviews when she circulated the manuscript to family and friends. She quickly realized that the book wasn't publishable. Undeterred, Egan stuck with her original idea but rewrote the book. The result was her debut novel, *The Invisible Circus*.

First drafts have tormented many great writers throughout history. Harper Lee was among this troubled set. On a cold winter night, New York City pedestrians may have seen draft pages of *To Kill a Mockingbird* as they fluttered down from Lee's apartment window and onto the snow-covered ground. In a fit of despair, she had actually defenestrated her manuscript. Luckily, Lee's editor was able to convince the frustrated author to go outside and rescue her book.

There's always a slim chance that a failed manuscript might be transformed, if left alone for enough time. Stephen King's *The Cannibals* was five hundred pages long when he decided to give up on the book. He moved on to other novels, and *The Cannibals* lay dormant for many years. Then, almost three decades later, he took another stab at the book, only this time he added a different twist to the story. The new version, *Under the Dome*, was published in 2009.

Sometimes there is no saving a book. Junot Díaz and Michael Chabon are among literary greats who abandoned entire novels that weren't working. Thomas Hardy's first manuscript was rejected several times and never made it to publication. Toward the end of his career, Hardy had given up completely on the book. He destroyed the manuscript.

Evelyn Waugh had a wretched time launching his career. A negative review of Waugh's first manuscript prompted the fledgling author to attempt suicide. He survived (and so did his literary career), but the poorly received manuscript did not.

Assembly Puzzling

VLADIMIR NABOKOV

1899–1977

*I fill in the gaps of the crossword at any spot
I happen to choose.*

—Vladimir Nabokov,
in an interview for the *Paris Review*

Vladimir Nabokov's home in his final years was Montreux Palace, a Swiss hotel. An insomniac, Nabokov was prone to waking throughout the night. If he did stir and found that a new idea had sprouted in his dreams, he would reach underneath his pillow. There, like a token to the literary muses, was a stack of lined Bristol note cards. Nabokov could record the idea on one of the three-by-five rectangles before it evaporated.

In his twenties and thirties, Nabokov had worked in bed, puffing away on cigarettes and contemplating one lyrical sentence after the next. Throughout the years, the cigarettes were replaced with molasses candy, resulting in inevitable weight gain. His physical position also changed over time: At the hotel in Switzerland, during his sixties and seventies, Nabokov began the workday on his feet.

Though inspiration sometimes arrived unpredictably during restless nights, Nabokov kept a steady schedule in his hotel home. He started the day at a lectern that had been plucked from the hotel basement. When Nabokov grew tired, he moved to an armchair. And, finally, when his back needed a rest, he stretched out horizontally on a couch. Nabokov described the shifting positions as "a pleasant solar routine." From rise to set, the note cards were a constant tool.

Nabokov originally used note cards for scientific rather than literary purposes. An enthusiastic lepidopterologist, he embarked on annual expeditions in search of rare specimens. The small, sturdy slips were ideal for maintaining observations about moths and butterflies. They were, it turns out, also perfectly suited for Nabokov's creative process. In his early fifties, he used note cards to draft *Lolita*, which would become his most famous work.

Nabokov let a novel simmer in his mind, waiting for a full picture to develop, before setting to work on the manuscript. In the meantime, he accumulated a broad assortment of details from various corners of his life. In an interview for *Playboy*, he described the hodgepodge as "known materials for an unknown structure." Interesting turns of phrase, brief descriptions, and observations were all recorded on note cards. Though Nabokov was not sure how each piece would lend itself to the work, he continued to assemble them, while the structure of the story was "uncurling inside."

Nabokov conducted extensive research for *Lolita*. He went as far as hopping on buses to listen to authentic conversations between American girls. Many other "unknown details" were assembled during lepidopteran trips. Nabokov was a professor at Cornell University, and on summer breaks, he set out across the western United States. Whether stopping at a run-down motel or passing through a small town, Nabokov soaked in the scenery. He recorded vivid images that later emerged in *Lolita*. And when it was difficult to find peace on the road, he shut himself in his car and wrote.

Once the framework of his story was mentally constructed, Nabokov picked up his pencil and started a new stack of note cards: the manuscript. Rather than building his novel linearly, he swooped in from all angles. The process was, he observed, like working on a crossword puzzle. He wrote and rewrote, often exhausting an eraser before its pencil. After filling in a note card, he slipped it into the pile according to where it fit within the story. Even then the note cards might be rearranged. So he waited until the manuscript was complete before numbering each one.

Lolita grew at a painstakingly slow pace, and in a low moment, Nabokov decided to burn the manuscript. His wife, Véra, suggested that he not take such drastic action. He took her advice and continued to forge through the book. Véra also helped Nabokov transcribe his note cards. He depended on her to type his work, having never learned the skill himself. Nabokov dictated *Lolita* to Véra during a trip to Oregon. Three note cards translated to one typed page. (One of Nabokov's longer novels, *Ada*, consisted of twenty-five hundred note cards.)

Nabokov knew *Lolita*, about an older man falling in love with a young girl, would cause some uproar. He even considered using a pseudonym. Because the material was so controversial, Nabokov also decided to get rid of his note cards, leaving fewer links back to him. After the pages were typed, the *Lolita* cards were immediately dispersed in a direct reflection of their assembly. Earlier, Nabokov had drawn inspiration for his book on long drives. Now the same cards that held those ideas flew from the car window and onto the road. Other note cards were dropped into motel fireplaces, in the same type of setting where many of them were originally inscribed. Only one hundred note cards with Nabokov's early observations survived, along with the typewritten manuscript (which was ultimately published under the author's real name).

Bath Time

As a young father, Vladimir Nabokov combined work with baths. Nap times were particularly productive for the stay-at-home dad. While his son slept, Nabokov sat in the bath with a writing board positioned above the water and wrote. Years later, he still incorporated the bathtub into his writing regimen. He required a morning bath every day before work. When asked about his "principle failing as a writer" in an interview for *Playboy*, Nabokov cited, among other things, an "inability to express myself properly in any language unless I compose every damned sentence in my bath, in my mind, at my desk." (Nabokov first wrote in Russian, his native language, but shifted to English in 1940.)

Many writers, in addition to Nabokov, have stepped into their tubs with pen and paper in hand. Somerset Maugham put his morning bath time to good use. While immersed in water, he would conjure his first two sentences of the day.

Edmond Rostand, playwright of *Cyrano de Bergerac*, sought refuge in the bathtub. When inspiration sparked for him, it crackled and roared rather than fading into an ember. In order to avoid any interruption during bouts of intense creativity, he took daylong baths. Rostand informed the French diplomat Madame de Hegermann-Lindencrone that he wrote his play *L'Aiglon* while submerged in water. He was proud of his unusual work space. "I consider my idea is rather original!" he remarked.

Benjamin Franklin spent hours soaking in luxuriously hot water in his copper bathtub. While the steam drifted up, he read, wrote, and relaxed. Franklin also took a daily "tonic bath." This consisted of shedding his clothes as soon as he woke up. He sat naked, working in his room, for up to an hour.

When Agatha Christie was planning to renovate her mansion, Greenway House, she said to architect Guilford Bell, "I want a big bath and I need a ledge because I like to eat apples." These requests were essential for the author whose bathroom was also a prime work area. Relaxing in a large Victorian bathtub, Christie devised brilliant plots one bite at a time. Her progress, or at least time spent at work, was marked by the apple cores left on the wooden ledge that surrounded the lip of the tub.

Diane Ackerman finds creative liberation in the suds. "One summer, lolling in baths, I wrote an entire verse play," she recalled. Junot Díaz is another contemporary author who finds inspiration in the bathroom. Rather than getting into the tub, he sits on the side and composes his work. "It drove my ex crazy," he observed.

Díaz's discord would have intensified dramatically had he followed Dorothy Parker's example. Parker didn't write in the bathtub, but she found a unique use for it. She gave two small alligators a temporary home in her tub. She had spotted the pair in a New York taxicab and promptly took them back to her apartment. The tub was quick thinking on Parker's part. However, she forgot to tell someone about her new pets. The maid encountered the sharp-toothed, beady-eyed reptiles when Parker was out. She left her boss a note that read: "Dear Madam. I am leaving, as I cannot work in a house with alligators. I would have told you this before, but I never thought the subject would come up."

Outstanding Prose

ERNEST HEMINGWAY
1899–1961

*Once writing has become your major vice and
greatest pleasure only death can stop it.*

—Ernest Hemingway,
in an interview for the *Paris Review*

In January 1954, Ernest Hemingway was in a tiny plane soaring over the Nile River. The author had booked an aerial tour as a Christmas present for Mary, his fourth wife. While they were admiring the landscape, a flock of ibises appeared directly in the plane's path. The quick-thinking pilot, Roy Marsh, steered down to avoid the birds, but unfortunately caught an old telegraph wire in the process. They suffered some injuries in the emergency landing, but none were fatal (the worst was Mary's broken ribs).

However, their rescue from the rural crash exacerbated

the injuries. Another pilot, Reginald Cartwright, discovered the small party, packed them into his plane, and proceeded to take off. But after a few seconds, the plane plummeted back to the ground. Hemingway had to head butt a jammed door to escape, and with greater urgency this time, as a fire was filling the interior with smoke.

Hemingway suffered several injuries in the second crash, including damage to his spine. From then on, long bouts of sitting could be excruciating for him. So, according to several journalists and scholars, in 1954, after Hemingway returned to his home in Cuba, he wrote standing up. However, Hemingway must have written while standing at least intermittently before the crash. He humorously mentioned the benefits of standing on the job in a letter to reviewer Harvey Breit that predates the Africa trip by approximately four years. Hemingway observed, "Writing and travel broaden your ass if not your mind and I like to write standing up."

Hemingway's Cuban home was called *Finca Vigía*, which means "Lookout Farm." Though he had his own study in a tall tower at the side of the house, Hemingway chose to write in the comfort of his bedroom. He created a special work area to accommodate his creative process. A midsize bookcase that faced the wall served as the writing surface. Piles of books and papers lined the shelf on either side of his typewriter. Hemingway would stand in comfortable loafers and lean down on the top shelf to work. On the wall, beneath a stuffed gazelle head, sat a word count chart.

Hemingway typically added around five hundred words to the chart daily.

Hemingway's routine in Cuba began with an early start to the day. He allocated the entire morning to writing, working from around 6:30 a.m. to noon. Hemingway would eat breakfast in his bedroom while he worked. During these hours, some of his beloved pets kept him company. At one point, there were about fifty cats and a dozen dogs at *Finca Vigía*. Hemingway's favorite four-legged friends were Black Dog, a springer spaniel, and Boise, a cat (see page 77). He wrote about Black Dog in a letter to Breit: "He knows my writing is in some way connected to sizzling steaks so he spends all his time getting me to the typewriter."

Thornton Wilder claimed that Hemingway began each workday by sharpening twenty pencils. In a later interview with George Plimpton for the *Paris Review*, Hemingway refuted the notion of even owning that many pencils. He stated, "Wearing down seven number-two pencils is a good day's work."

Still, pencils were undisputedly Hemingway's favorite medium for his first drafts. He observed, "If you write with a pencil you get three different sights at it to see if the reader is getting what you want him to. First when you read it over; then when it is typed you get another chance to improve it, and again in the proof. Writing it first in pencil gives you one-third more chance to improve it."

Perhaps one of Hemingway's most important writing

maxims was to step away from his desk before his inspiration ran dry. He described his process to Plimpton: "You write until you come to a place where you still have your juice and know what will happen next and you stop and try to live through until the next day when you hit it again." When he arrived at his stack of paper the next morning, Hemingway would revise the latest addition to the story. Then, when he came to the point where he'd left off, he knew what was about to happen next. He observed, "As long as you can start, you are all right. The juice will come."

In *I'll Always Have Paris*, journalist Art Buchwald described another solution Hemingway had for writer's block. Buchwald recalled that a friend of his, upon meeting Hemingway, asked him what one needed to do to become a writer. According to Buchwald, Hemingway informed the aspiring writer, "First, you have to defrost the refrigerator."

Sound Writing

JOHN STEINBECK
1902–1968

I know how I want it to sound and I know how I want it to feel.

–John Steinbeck, on *East of Eden*,
in a letter to editor Pascal Covici

John Steinbeck was just a young boy when he had a life-altering revelation. He realized that "high" rhymes with "fly." The interplay between sound and meaning was marvelous to him. The enthralled four-year-old was destined to become a wordsmith.

By the time he reached high school, Steinbeck was composing stories, and he was preoccupied with how they sounded out loud. Steinbeck's neighbor proved to be the perfect test audience. Not only did Lucille Hughes appreciate the art of writing, she was also conveniently located across the street. Hughes was good friends with Steinbeck's mother, Olive, though it is likely she saw more of the bold teen during his junior and senior years.

Hughes was not fond of Steinbeck, but he didn't seem to notice. He would arrive on her doorstep, stride into her home, and read his work aloud. These readings took place even if Hughes was busy with housework, which was usually the case. Though she was exasperated by the frequent interruptions, Hughes always offered an honest critique. She did not hesitate to inform Steinbeck that he needed to simplify his vocabulary. So Steinbeck began, with the help of a reluctant neighbor, to sound out his stories. The spoken word remained central to his writing process throughout his career.

At twenty-seven, Steinbeck described the physical act of writing as a mere by-product of his desire to tell a story. In a letter to A. Grove Day, a writer he met at Stanford University, Steinbeck declared, "I would continue to write if there were no writing and no print. I put my words down for a matter of memory." Steinbeck was responding to Day's claim that writers should deliver a pristine manuscript to the publisher. Though Steinbeck's debut, *Cup of Gold*, had only been released five months earlier, he argued with the conviction of a seasoned writer. He observed, "There are millions of people who are good stenographers but there aren't so many thousands who can make as nice sounds as I can."

The budding author saw himself as a "minstrel" and not a "scrivener." He preferred to focus on the telling of a story and let someone else clean up the grammar and spelling.

Steinbeck's finely tuned ear must have come in handy when he wrote *Of Mice and Men*. The novella was designed to function as a book and a script. Steinbeck noted, "I wanted to call it at first 'a play to be read.'" As the scenes unfolded on the page, Steinbeck was also envisioning them on the stage. The end of each chapter signaled the fall of a curtain.

Of Mice and Men was published in January of 1937. Soon after the release of the book, playwright and director George S. Kaufman informed Steinbeck that he wanted to bring the tale to the stage. Kaufman's production was a hit. Despite its undisputable success (the play ran for 207 performances on Broadway), Steinbeck considered his "playable novel" a failure. Steinbeck lamented that the book didn't adapt seamlessly into a script: "The experiment flopped. By that I mean when I came up against a practical man of the theatre like Kaufman I found that I had to do a lot more extensive rewriting of the book itself." However, it seems that Steinbeck was a tough critic. He had actually almost hit his mark, as the majority of the story and the dialogue were not altered for the production.

The image of a writer at work usually involves a person hunched over a desk, poring over pages of work. In

Steinbeck's case, there would be a Dictaphone by the stack of paper. In 1942, Steinbeck was commissioned to write a nonfiction book for the air force, and he was under a very tight deadline. So, he informed his friend Toby Street, "I'm dictating a book into the ediphone." The recording device helped him work faster, and he found that he preferred a machine to the human alternative. He reflected, "I always have a feeling that I am keeping a steno from going home and doing what she wants to. But this machine is a slave and has no rights nor any home." *Bombs Away: The Story of a Bomber Team* raced to completion at the rapid clip of four thousand words per day (a rate that even alarmed Steinbeck to a degree).

Four years later Steinbeck switched on a Dictaphone to draft his novel *The Wayward Bus*. On a standard workday he would descend into the basement of his home on the Upper East Side of Manhattan. In this quiet refuge, he wrote letters and journal entries before proceeding to the manuscript. His goal was to fill three pages on a yellow legal pad.

Steinbeck preferred to compose his drafts in pencil, for the most part. He kept twelve pencils at his desk, and it was essential that each one had a sharp point. An electric pencil sharpener was one of his most cherished tools. Steinbeck summed up his work regimen: "I sharpen all the pencils in the morning and it takes one more sharpening for a day's work. That's twenty-four sharp points. I can make a newly sharpened pencil last almost a page." With such prolific output, he often developed calluses on his fingers. His thoughtful editor sent him round pencils to alleviate the pain inflicted by hexagonal ones.

After he had written his draft in longhand, Steinbeck then dictated it into his machine. He'd play it back for review, closing his eyes to get the full effect of the work. After incorporating revisions to the manuscript, Steinbeck recorded a revised version for the stenographer to type. This process of dictation apparently helped speed up Steinbeck's work once again; he finished the novel two months before his projected deadline.

Steinbeck's Dictaphone was a fixture in his study long after he finished *The Wayward Bus*. During an interview in 1958, he spoke about his writing process (at this point he had completed more than twenty books). He noted that the first draft was written in pencil and the second was recorded on the Dictaphone. Some of Steinbeck's best revision occurred while listening to the prose. "You can hear the most terrible things you've done if you hear it clear back on tape," he explained. The recordings lifted his words right off the page. Steinbeck had tried reading aloud, but it didn't offer the necessary distance. "Then," he noted, "my eyes are involved."

When asked who his influences were as a youth, Steinbeck named two authors: Donn Byrne and James Branch

Cabell. He added, "These men were specialists in sound—and that's what I was after." Steinbeck did precisely what he set out to do: specializing in sound—from reading aloud to his neighbor as a teenager to listening to his voice on tape years later.

Speak Up

John Steinbeck wasn't the only author to talk his way into great literature. Several renowned writers were compelled, for one reason or another, to put down their pens and dictate their work.

* After he lost his sight, John Milton turned to those around him to serve as amanuenses. He dictated his epic poem *Paradise Lost* to a variety of people, including friends, family members, and students. The poet called upon visitors to record stanzas, whether committed to memory or composed on the spot.

* William Makepeace Thackeray dictated his prose to his eldest daughter, Anne. However, she recalled that when her father "came to a critical point he would send his secretary away and write for himself."

* When the due date loomed for his novel *The Gambler*, Fyodor Dostoyevsky took on a stenographer to save time. Twenty-year-old Anna Grigorievna Snitkina got the job. Together, they raced to complete the book within one month. The writer and the stenographer proved to be a perfect pair: They met the deadline and fell in love. After they were married, Dostoyevsky continued to dictate novels to his wife.

* In 1897, painful rheumatism drove fifty-three-year-old Henry James to find an alternative to the typewriter. For the rest of his life, he relied on amanuenses to compose letters and novels. Theodora Bosanquet, one of James's typists, recalled how particular he was about the sound of a typewriter. "He dictated to an Oliver typewriter with evident discomfort, and found it impossibly disconcerting to write to something that made no responsive sound at all," noted Bosanquet. A Remington, however, produced the perfect clack.

Pin It Down

EUDORA WELTY

1909–2001

*That's what I really love doing—putting things
in their best and proper place, revealing things
at the time when they matter most.*

—Eudora Welty, in an interview
for the *Paris Review*

Eudora Welty evaluated her work with scissors handy. If anything needed to be moved, she cut it right out of the page.
Then she'd use pins to put the section in its new place. In
a letter to author and editor William Maxwell, Welty listed
an assortment of pins that she used for one of her novels.
She recalled, "*The Ponder Heart* was in straight pins, hat pins,
corsage pins, and needles, and when I got through typing it
out, I had more pins than I started with. (So it's economi-
cal.)" Welty also liked the flexibility of revising with pins. In

an interview for the *Paris Review,* she observed that if glue was used, "you can't undo it." Pins made it easy to move a snippet of text again and again.

Welty would place her altered pages on her bed or the dining room table. When she was done cutting and pinning, she sat down and typed a clean version. The freshly typed pages were then subject to another round of cutting and pinning. And some sections underwent several rounds of revision.

Welty composed most of her work in Jackson, Mississippi, the town where she grew up. Though she loved to travel, she always returned to her hometown. During her senior year of high school, Welty's family moved into a charming house on Pinehurst Street in Jackson. As the eldest of six children, Welty had the honor of picking a prime bedroom on the second floor. Welty left Jackson to attend college, first in Mississippi and later in New York. She tried a few times to find a literary job in Manhattan, with no luck. Eventually, in her late twenties, Welty settled back in that same house on Pinehurst Street, where her mother, Chestina, still lived (Welty's father passed away in 1931).

Welty's typical workday began in the morning, while she was still in her nightgown. She would sit at her desk in the second-floor bedroom that she had selected as a teen. Though she faced the wall, she preferred to work in close proximity to the outside view. So, as she wrote, sunlight would filter in from the window to her side. She noted, "I like to be aware of the world going on while I'm working." Welty's first drafts were written directly on a typewriter. "I guess my journalistic training taught me to want to see something on the page, objective, in type," she observed. After college, she had briefly worked as a journalist.

Before she placed her fingers on the typewriter keys to compose a story, Welty compiled all sorts of notes in a stenographer pad. In fact, when Chestina was in a convalescent home sixty miles away, Welty would make the long drive with a pad by her side. As soon as an idea struck, she'd scribble it down without pulling over. Her friends were understandably concerned about the unsafe habit. Still, she always made it home safely with the new ideas that were recorded en route. It seems, wherever she was, Welty was compelled to write down ideas as soon as they arrived. And yet, once those notes were distilled into prose, they were subject to the slow, fine art of revision with pins that she developed over the years.

When an interviewer asked Welty to describe the origin of her "pins-and-scissors method," she offered two explanations, one related to sewing and the other to journalism. First, she said, "Did you ever cut and make dresses from patterns? Well, I guess it's that that made me think of it." Though she was never a proficient seamstress, Welty had witnessed the practice of sewing firsthand. Chestina would cut fabric for her children's dresses and outfits. Then a woman named Fannie would visit the Welty's home and assemble the attire on-site.

Welty also traced her method back to her short-lived career in journalism. In that fast-paced environment, journalists used long scrolls of paper to type their work. Welty had learned to tear any prose that wasn't working right off the typewriter. Then she'd adjust the torn page and continue writing. She added, "Except I was too prudent, I guess, to really throw it away. I would save it in case I might need it after all. So I had these strips."

Welty became aware of the importance of revision while reading her work aloud to an audience. As she stood before a crowd and spoke, she often noticed areas in her stories that needed improvement. While discussing her readings at colleges, Welty recalled, "I could see all these weaknesses that had been in there all these years and I didn't know it." These weaknesses frequently involved a simple shift, moving a piece of a story from one place to another. Welty repeatedly found that something in the beginning of a story fit much better at the end. She remarked, "It's possible I have a reverse mind, and do things backwards, being a broken left-hander."

Each change, no matter how minute, seemed to impact Welty with the same immediate urgency as the original ideas that she jotted in her stenographer pads. Welty observed, "It's strange how in revision you find some little unconsidered thing which is so essential that you not only keep it in but give it preeminence when you revise." Sometimes, late at night, while she lay in bed, Welty would realize a particular change that needed to be made. When this nocturnal revelation occurred, she'd make a quick note to remind her of what to address the next day.

Night and day, Welty's thoughts wandered to her fiction. And, though she was never skilled at sewing her clothes, Welty was, in her own literary way, a master seamstress. She was constantly snipping, pinning, and adjusting her text, striving to find the best fit for a word, sentence, or paragraph within the framework of a story.

Point of View

Eudora Welty wasn't the only writer who preferred to face away from a window. Ernest Hemingway's work space in Havana, Cuba, was on the top shelf of a bookcase in his bedroom. He would stand facing the wall, first writing in pencil before moving to his typewriter (see page 132).

Flannery O'Connor placed her desk against the back of an armoire to maintain her focus. The view of plain wood was far less distracting than the country landscape outside her bedroom window (see page 160).

When John Steinbeck lived on East 78th Street in Manhattan, he used his basement as a writer's studio. The author was happy to avoid the distraction of the bustling city. He maintained, "No window, no ability to look out and watch the postman and the garbage wagon."

Maya Angelou uses more extreme methods to avoid distraction. No matter where she is residing, Angelou finds a local hotel and rents out a room to write in. She asks that everything be removed from the walls to help her focus completely on writing. In an interview with Angelou for the *Paris Review*, George Plimpton listed the select items that the author kept in her otherwise spartan work environment: "a bottle of sherry, a dictionary, *Roget's Thesaurus*, yellow pads, an ashtray, and a Bible."

In terms of intense focus, few spaces come close to the one where Dame Edith Sitwell lay every morning. Diane Ackerman reported that Sitwell found inspiration in extraordinarily tight quarters. Before she set pen to paper, the poet would lie in an open coffin. There, in that windowless setting, she prepared for her day's work.

When he turned fifty, George Bernard Shaw moved to a small town called Ayot St. Lawrence, where he worked in a tiny shed in his backyard. He faced a wooden wall, but there were windows on either side. Shaw rigged his shed so that it would rotate. That way, rather than lamenting the way the light fell into his room, he could adjust his position whenever he liked.

On the other end of the spectrum, in terms of a view, was Mark Twain. His sister-in-law had an idyllic writing room built for him on a hilltop on Quarry Hill, her farm in Elmira, New York. Twain and his family spent summers at the farm. The isolated writing quarters suited Twain perfectly. Every day, he strolled out to his special hut, which was located far away from the general hubbub on the farm. Twain described the space: "It is octagonal, with a peaked roof, each face filled with a spacious window, and it sits perched in complete isolation on the top of an elevation that commands leagues of valley and city and retreating ranges of distant blue hills. It is a cozy nest." As he wrote, Twain could look up in any direction and take in the beautiful panorama, before setting back to work.

Don't Get Up

TRUMAN CAPOTE

1924–1984

I can't think unless I'm lying down.

—Truman Capote in an interview
for the *Paris Review*

Truman Capote was in his creative element when fully re-
clined. He stated, "I'm a completely horizontal author."
Capote's workday began in the same place where one typically ends—lying in bed or on a couch. He'd rest a notebook against his knees and write. A cup of coffee and a
cigarette were always positioned within reach. "I've got to
be puffing and sipping," he observed. Over the course of
the day, Capote's position remained the same, but his bever-
ages changed. After coffee, he transitioned to mint tea, followed by sherry. By the end of the day, he'd have a martini
in hand.

Capote wrote his first two drafts in pencil and didn't get up to type the third round. He placed a typewriter on his knees and, despite the uneven surface, still managed to transcribe his work onto yellow paper at the impressive rate of one hundred words a minute. The manuscript was then set aside. Capote decided the fate of the work with fresh eyes sometime later. If he wanted to submit the piece for publication, he typed it once more on white paper.

With each round of revision, Capote evaluated his prose with the eye of a master craftsman. He considered every little detail, right down to the punctuation marks. From the inner workings of a sentence to the framework of the story, Capote staged each part of his manuscript with great care. Early in his career, he used detailed outlines, though eventually he found there was no need for that step; a good idea would stick in his mind. "I've always had the illusion that a story or a novel springs into my mind *in toto*—plot, characters, scenes, dialog, everything—in one long rush," he noted. Still, he did prefer to write the final pages before he was well under way. The ending, like a cardinal point, helped guide him to the final destination.

Capote warned, "We must be on guard against that feverish state called inspiration, which is often a matter of nerves rather than muscle. Everything should be done coldly, with poise." And yet it seems that an unexpected burst of creativity—the "one long rush"—was an essential counterbalance to Capote's orderly procedure. Some of his best books were set into motion with a great big spark. And he was fully aware of the importance of being steered, to a degree, by a wave of inspiration.

During the winter of 1944, Capote was midway through his first novel when he decided to abandon it. He was walking through the wilderness in Monroeville, Alabama, when the idea for a new novel struck. The creative flash was so disorienting that he had trouble finding his way home. When he did get back, he raced upstairs, and began to work "with pathetic optimism." The result was his *New York Times* best-selling debut, *Other Voices, Other Rooms*.

While in Monroeville, Capote adopted a routine of working in bed in the middle of the night. He was living with his aunts at the time. They questioned his schedule in a caring yet overbearing way. He recalled their criticism: "But you've got everything turned upside down. You're ruining your health." Their constant watch drove Capote to move to New Orleans, where he could work wherever and whenever he pleased. But, after only a few months, he moved up to Manhattan to live with his mother, Nina, and stepfather, Joe Capote. He remained an "upside-down" author in each place, composing his scenes from around 10 p.m. to 4 a.m., while most people slept.

Like his debut, Capote's "nonfiction novel" *In Cold Blood* also began with a sudden jolt of inspiration. In November 1959, Capote was flipping through the *New York Times* when he stumbled across a brief article. With spare detail, it told of a ruthless murder in the small town of Holcomb, Kansas. Capote was hooked immediately. He promptly contacted an editor at the *New Yorker* to pitch a piece about the crime. Capote got the assignment, raced out to the Midwest, and began to work on an article that would evolve into an epic book.

By the time he wrote *In Cold Blood*, Capote had shifted to writing in the daytime. His schedule would certainly have met his aunts' approval, though one can only imagine their response to his cycle of coffee, tea, sherry, and martinis. And, despite the fact that this new routine could be described by his relatives as "right side up," Capote, true to his character, still deviated from the norm by writing while lying down.

Off the Recorder

A tape recording can help or, according to a couple of renowned writers, hinder the creative process. Truman Capote never brought a tape recorder to the countless interviews he conducted for *In Cold Blood*. He didn't even carry a notebook. Capote asserted, "If you erect any kind of mechanical barrier, it destroys the mood and inhibits people from talking freely." The writer relied on a photographic memory to retain the facts, which were promptly recorded on paper post-interview. His childhood friend Harper Lee also lent a hand with the interviews, and they compared notes to confirm details.

William S. Burroughs used tape recorders for literary experiments, but he thought dictation was an unnecessary, painstaking process. He noted, "I never used a tape recorder to compose onto it—it's a waste of time. It's more trouble to take it off a tape recorder than it is to put it on a typewriter to begin with."

Gay Talese blamed the downfall of journalism on the

tape recorder. He condemned the device as "number one the worst thing that ever happened to serious non-fiction writing." Talese believed tape recorders reduced interviews to questions and answers. He preferred to follow his subjects from place to place, and even outdoors, in order to assemble complex portraits.

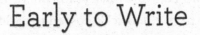

Early to Write

FLANNERY O'CONNOR

1925–1964

If I waited for inspiration, I'd still be waiting.

—Flannery O'Connor, on her daily writing habit,
in an interview for the *Atlanta Journal and
Constitution Magazine*, October 1959

A schedule is nothing new in the writing world. It's important to find the best time to work, whether that means juggling a hectic lifestyle or pinpointing the hour one is most creative. But few people are able to stick with the same time slot for most of their lives, even fewer on a daily basis. Flannery O'Connor set aside three hours every morning to write and almost never skipped a day. Her ritual was woven so tightly into her life that it was as natural and necessary as eating a meal or taking a next breath.

During the 1950s, O'Connor lived in a white farmhouse

a few miles outside Milledgeville, Georgia. The house was located at the end of a dirt road, where peacocks often roamed (see page 49). Brick steps led to a wide front porch, which was lined with rocking chairs. Through a screen door and to the left was O'Connor's bedroom. Every morning, every single day of the week, the slender author with striking blue eyes would sit down in that room and write.

O'Connor began each day by attending an early mass. Then she would retreat to a sanctuary of a different sort. O'Connor's small bedroom doubled as a study. It contained two large windows, but she opted to face away from the glass. O'Connor planted her desk directly behind an armoire. When the devout writer looked up from her work, the view was plain and static. The blank panels of wood were a constant, as opposed to the shifting landscape of the farm.

O'Connor's desk was a makeshift piece of furniture, which she described in a letter to her close friend Betty Hester. (An insightful fan letter from Hester was the catalyst for their lifelong friendship.) O'Connor wrote, "I have a large ugly brown desk, one of those that a typewriter sits in a depression in the middle of and on either side are drawers. In front I have a stained mahogany orange crate with the bottom knocked out and a cartridge shell box that I have sat up there to lend height." A plank of wood connected the improvised shelves. Scattered all over the desk were papers, notes, and articles that offered inspiration.

It may seem surprising that O'Connor's work space did

not fall into the same order as her strict schedule, but she was not at all rigid when it came to the act of writing. Her stories evolved rather than adhering to a careful outline. She observed, "I just kind of feel [the story] out like a hound-dog. I follow the scent." Inspiration was not something she could plan, which is precisely why she needed her daily ritual. O'Connor had to be ready, fingers near the typewriter. That way she could be certain, she noted, "if anything comes I am there waiting to receive it."

O'Connor worked slowly rather than in large bursts. Every morning, during her unvarying appointment, she inched forward line by line, fell back several pages, and crept forward again. She wrote about three pages per sitting, sometimes less, and often discarded her work the following day. O'Connor valued each page, whether it was tossed or kept, as an important part of the creative process. In a letter to Cecil Dawkins, she wrote, "Sometimes I work for months and have to throw everything away, but I don't think any of that was time wasted. Something goes on that makes it easier when it does come well. And the fact is that if you don't sit there every day, the day it would come well, you won't be sitting there."

O'Connor kept to that same regimen every day, even on weekends, for the majority of her adult life. And yet she did not fall into it with ease. She admitted, "The discipline doesn't come naturally to me, but I've had to develop it." There was a turning point, when O'Connor decided to adopt the strict schedule, or at least work toward it, and she was far from her home state when it took place.

Twenty-year-old O'Connor arrived at the University of Iowa as a graduate student intending to study journalism. It quickly became apparent that she was far better suited to creative writing, and she changed her major accordingly. O'Connor did not adapt well to the northern environment. Cold winters were a shock to the Georgia native, and she felt desperately homesick. Her Southern twang was incomprehensible to students and professors alike. When asked to read one of her stories aloud, O'Connor would hand the piece to a fellow student—preferably, to maintain a sense of her voice, another Southerner—but one with a less powerful drawl.

Despite her outsider status, O'Connor developed significantly as a writer in Iowa. It was there she learned one of the most important—and perhaps simplest and most straightforward—lessons of her life. It was a nugget of wisdom passed along by her Imaginative Writing professor, Paul Horgan. He advised her to pick a time and place to write every day, and she decided to adopt this simple practice.

O'Connor mastered her daily schedule as a graduate and postgraduate student at the University of Iowa. Every morning, when many other students slept in, she went to mass and then returned to her bedroom to write. During this time, she developed several short stories, including "The Geranium" and "The Train." It may not have been easy at first, but eventually the routine became a daily habit that stayed with her wherever she went, from city to city, through sickness and health.

After she left Iowa, O'Connor spent almost a year at Yaddo, an artist's colony in Saratoga Springs, New York. She then followed her friend and writing advocate Robert Lowell to New York City, the epicenter of the publishing world. The metropolis was bustling and chaotic, but O'Connor did not let it interfere with her schedule: first mass, then a stretch of writing, as she plugged away at her debut novel, *Wise Blood*. After six months in the city, O'Connor moved to rural Connecticut to live with Robert and Sally Fitzgerald.

O'Connor's room was perched above the Fitzgeralds' garage. It was a peaceful location and the rent was cheap. Every morning O'Connor attended mass with Sally or Robert, who were also devout Catholics, and then she wrote, with her attention fixed on the developing novel. All she had to do in exchange for the ideal setup was babysit in the afternoons, and by that time, she was already done writing for the day. Finally, O'Connor had settled into a place that felt like home, but her cozy life up north was short-lived. After a year and a half with the Fitzgeralds, she was forced to move back to Georgia.

When she was twenty-five, O'Connor was diagnosed with lupus. The degenerative disease had killed her father in his forties and it would now alter the course of her life. She battled sickness (which, at first, she did not know was lupus) for more than a year, planning to move back to Connecticut once she regained her strength. Unfortunately, it became clear that O'Connor would need help to survive. The young writer moved onto a dairy farm with her mother, Regina. She dubbed the place Andalusia and lived there for the rest of her life.

O'Connor was forced to use aluminum crutches as the disease worsened. Lupus targeted her hips, making it difficult to walk, but it did not weaken her fierce spirit. In an interview for the *Atlanta Journal and Constitution Magazine*, O'Connor stated, "The disease is of no consequence to my writing, since for that I use my head and not my feet." She maintained her routine despite the chronic pain that came with lupus.

Soon after she arrived at Andalusia, O'Connor secured a publisher (Harcourt, Brace & Company) for *Wise Blood*. The novel was published in 1952 without widespread fanfare, but it marked a positive shift in her career. She would, from that point on, be regarded not only as a short story writer, but a novelist, too. Over the years, she produced another novel and two short story collections, and her morning routine charted the steady heartbeat of this literary life. With each thrum, she inched forward, slowly and meticulously creating a body of work that was by no means prolific and yet, since its publication, has received much critical attention.

When O'Connor was thirty-nine, she was admitted to a

hospital. The lupus had grown worse. Though her body had started to fail her, O'Connor's mind was alive and spirited. All she wanted was to write. O'Connor informed a friend, "The doctor says I mustn't do any work. But he says it's all right for me to write a little fiction." So the stubborn author hid a notebook under her pillow, gleefully extracting it when the nurses were out of sight. That way, she was able to sneak in extra work, along with letters to friends. There was no way she was able to stick with her cherished routine during those days, which proved to be her last. Still, rather than letting go, she forged ahead. The literary thrum that was once a series of steady mornings became a flutter: erratic, stolen moments that allowed her to, in her own way, exist.

Sweet Teeth

Flannery O'Connor did not smoke while clacking on typewriter keys, though many of her contemporaries did. The Southern writer preferred to indulge her sweet tooth. According to Jean Williams, a friend from the University of Iowa, O'Connor "nibbled on cookies while she wrote." Vanilla wafers to be exact.

Unlike O'Connor, short story master Raymond Carver suffered from common literary vices. He smoked cigarettes and drank alcohol for decades (finally giving up drinking in his late thirties). But he shared with O'Connor a penchant for sweet food. He devoured Fiddle Faddle (candy-coated popcorn with nuts), along with doughnuts, brownies, and cookies. And to drink? Coca-Cola and ginger ale.

Ray Bradbury's self-prescribed treatment for nerves was ice cream. During the proof stages of his novel *Fahrenheit 451*, Bradbury began to question elements of the book. Stanley Kauffmann, his editor at the time, flew from New York to Los Angeles to help the panicked author in person. They holed up in Kauffmann's hotel room, worked through the proofs, and ate a lot of ice cream. Kauffmann recalled, "Well, I couldn't let him eat alone, so we both put on weight. I felt as if I were dealing with a giant of enthusiasm streaked with doubt that was subdued by ice cream, which I forced myself to eat in order to help him."

Acknowledgments

As I wrote a book about odd writers, I developed a habit of thinking about the oddities that, in part, define the people I care about most. After all, oddities aren't negative unless you cast them that way. In fact, the nuances that set us apart from one another are often our most superb attributes. For this book, I relied on a number of marvelously odd traits from the people around me.

Maria Gagliano, my friend, colleague, and constant advocate, is amazingly fierce and kind. She championed *Odd Type Writers* from the outset and paved a place for it on Perigee's list. My editor, Meg Leder, helped shape this book with extraordinary insight and patience. She offered support throughout the editorial process. I can't thank Maria and Meg enough for all of their efforts.

Nikki Van Noy, another dear friend and talented writer, took time to read my first draft. Her enthusiasm helped buoy me through revisions. I sincerely appreciate her willingness to lend a hand, no matter what time of day or day of the week it might be.

I wrote this book in the midst of a significant life change. I was midway through the manuscript when my husband, Ian, and I suddenly decided to pick up and move from Brooklyn to Maine. Ian and my daughter, Patricia, who was one at the time, both demonstrated tremendous patience as I danced between the computer screen and half-full boxes. Ian somehow managed to make a whirlwind move feel almost effortless. And, throughout it all, Patricia always made life fun, whether she was demanding to "read-a-booka" or to stomp in a pile of leaves outside.

We spent our first months in Maine living with my in-laws, Marsha and Scott McConnell. I am thankful to them for welcoming us into their home, which was a lovely writing retreat. My desk faced a window that looked out to row after row of tall deciduous trees. So, while my fingers raced across the computer keys, I could still look up and watch the seasons progress.

There's one person I have to thank above all: my mum. Trish Johnson is the most remarkable person I know. She helped me through this book in so many ways, it's impossible to pinpoint each one. Her inimitable sense of humor was a tremendous support. She can always elicit a laugh from me, with jokes that hinge on the truth rather than avoiding it. It turns out that a good chuckle is a fine cure for just about everything.

And, since I'm in an odd mood, I'd like to thank a few people who had virtually nothing to do with this book. But, in their own way, they kind of did. My brothers, C.J., Colin, and Christian, and my dad, Carl. We're so different, the members of my family, but we're a tight-knit group. Each one of those people helped make this book happen, simply by believing I could do it before I ever did.

Sources

Rotten Ideas: Friedrich Schiller

Carlyle, Thomas. *The Life of Friedrich Schiller*. London: Chapman and Hall, 1885.

Eckermann, Johann Peter. *Conversations of Goethe*. New York: Da Capo Press, 1998.

Nevinson, Henry Woodd, and John Parker Anderson. *Life of Friedrich Schiller*. London: Walter Scott, 1889.

Pilling, Claudia, Diana Schilling, and Mirjam Springer. *Schiller (Life and Times)*. Translated by Angus McGeoch. London: Haus Publishing, 2005.

Scherr, Johannes. *Schiller and His Times*. Philadelphia: Ig Kohler, 1880.

The Nightlife

Begley, Louis. *Franz Kafka: The Tremendous World Inside My Head*. New York: Atlas & Co. Publishers, 2008.

Carlyle, Thomas. *The Life of Friedrich Schiller*. London: Chapman and Hall, 1885.

Didion, Joan. "The Art of Fiction No. 71." Interview by Linda Kuehl. *Paris Review*, no. 74 (Fall–Winter 1978).

Fargnoli, A. Nicholas, Michael Golay, and Robert W. Hamblin. *Critical Companion to William Faulkner: A Literary Reference to His Life and Work*. New York: Facts on File, 2008.

Frost, Robert. *Interviews with Robert Frost*. Edited by Edward Connery Lathem. Madison, Connecticut: Jeffrey Norton Publishers, 1997.

Hamilton, Ian. *In Search of J. D. Salinger*. New York: Random House, 1988.

Kafka, Franz. *The Basic Kafka*. New York: Pocket Books, 1984.

Lewis Tuten, Nancy Zubizaretta, and John Zubizaretta, eds. *The Robert Frost Encyclopedia*. Westport: Greenwood Press, 2001.

Mochulsky, Konstantin. *Dostoevsky: His Life and Work*. Translated by Michael A. Minihan. Princeton: Princeton University Press, 1967.

Parini, Jay. *Robert Frost: A Life*. New York: Henry Holt and Company, 1999.

Wolfe, Tom. *Thomas Wolfe Interviewed 1929–1938*. Edited by Aldo P. Magi and Richard Walser. Baton Rouge: LSU Press, 1985.

By the Cup: Honoré de Balzac

De Balzac, Honoré. *The Correspondence of Honoré de Balzac with a Memoir by His Sister, Madame de Surville*. Vols. 1 and 2. Translated by C. Lamb Kenney. London: Richard Bentley and Son, 1878.

Keim, Albert, and Louis Lumet. *Honoré de Balzac*. Translated by Frederic Taber Cooper. New York: Frederick A. Stokes Company, 1914.

Robb, Graham. *Balzac: A Biography*. New York: W. W. Norton and Company, 1996.

Drinks with Inks

De Beauvoir, Simone. "The Art of Fiction No. 35." Interview by Madeleine Gobeil. *Paris Review*, no. 34 (Spring–Summer 1965).

Fitch, Noël Riley, and Andrew Midgley. *The Grand Literary Cafes of Europe*. London: New Holland Publishers, 2006.

Fox, Christopher. *The Cambridge Companion to Jonathan Swift*. New York: Cambridge University Press, 2003.

"A French Literary Café." *The Academy: A Weekly Review of Literature, Science, and Art*. Vol. 52–54 (July–October 1898).

Johnson, Samuel. *The Life of Pope*. New York: The Macmillan Company, 1899.

Lewis, C. S. *The Essential C. S. Lewis*. Edited by Lyle W. Dorsett. New York: Scribner, 1996.

———. *Of Other Worlds: Essays and Stories*. New York: Mariner Books, 2002.

Ukers, William Harrison. *All About Coffee*. New York: Tea and Coffee Trade Journal Company, 1922.

Feeling Blue: Alexandre Dumas, père

Davidson, Arthur Fitzwilliam. *Alexandre Dumas (père): His Life and Works*. Westminster: Archibald Constable & Co., 1902.

Dumas, Alexandre. *The Novels of Alexandre Dumas*. Translated by Alfred Allinson. London: Metheun & Co., 1904.

Manso, Peter. "Château d'If." Crime Museum. www.crimemuseum.org/library/imprisonment/chateauDIf.html.

Samuel, Henry. "Alexandre Dumas Novels Penned by 'Fourth Musketeer' Ghost Writer." *The Telegraph*. February 10, 2010. www.telegraph.co.uk/news/worldnews/europe/france/

7198679/Alexandre-Dumas-novels-penned-by-fourth-muske teer-ghost-writer.html.

Whidden, Seth Adam. *Models of Collaboration in Nineteenth-Century French Literature: Several Authors, One Pen*. London: Ashgate Publishing, 2009.

The Numbers Game

Carey, John. *William Golding: The Man Who Wrote* Lord of the Flies. London: Faber and Faber, 2009.

Cassis, A. F., ed. *Graham Greene: Man of Paradox*. Chicago: Loyola University Press, 1994.

Chandler, Raymond. *Raymond Chandler Speaking.* Edited by Dorothy Gardiner and Kathrine Sorley Walker. Los Angeles: University of California Press, 1997.

Coyle, John. *James Joyce: Ulysses/A Portrait of the Artist as a Young Man.* West Sussex: Columbia University Press, 1998.

Felbermann, Heinrich. *The Memoirs of a Cosmopolitan*. London: Chapman and Hall, 1936.

Fensch, Thomas. *Conversations with John Steinbeck.* Jackson: University Press of Mississippi, 1988.

Freedman, Carl. *Conversations with Isaac Asimov.* Jackson: University Press of Mississippi, 2005.

Hemmings, J. F. W. *Alexandre Dumas: The King of Romance.* New York: Scribner, 1979.

King, Stephen. *On Writing: A Memoir of the Craft.* New York: Scribner, 2010.

Manso, Peter. *Mailer: His Life and Times*. New York: Washington Square Press, 2008.

McCrum, Robert. *Wodehouse: A Life*. New York: Viking, 2004.

Parker, Dorothy. "The Art of Fiction No 13." Interview by Marion Capron. *Paris Review*, no. 113 (Summer 1956).

Stashower, Daniel. *Teller of Tales: The Life of Arthur Conan Doyle*. New York: Henry Holt and Company, 2001.

Thurber, James. "The Art of Fiction No. 10." Interview by George Plimpton and Max Steele. *Paris Review*, no. 10 (Fall 1955).

Trollope, Anthony. *An Autobiography*. New York: Oxford University Press, 2009.

Wolfe, Tom. "The Art of Fiction No. 123." Interview by George Plimpton. *Paris Review*, no. 118 (Spring 1991).

House Arrest: Victor Hugo

Barbou, Alfred. *Victor Hugo and His Time*. Translated by E. E. Frewer. London: Gilbert and Rivington, 1883.

Hugo, Adèle. *Victor Hugo: A Life Related by One Who Has Witnessed It*. Vol. 2. London: W. H. Allen & Co., 1863.

Hugo, Victor. *The Letters of Victor Hugo: To His Family, to Sainte-Beuve and Others*. Edited by Paul Meurice. Boston: Houghton, Mifflin and Company, 1896.

Josephson, Matthew. *Victor Hugo: A Realistic Biography of the Great Romantic*. New York: Jorge Pinto Books, 2006.

Mauris, Maurice. *French Men of Letters*. New York: D. Appleton and Company, 1901.

Taking It in Stride

Bell, Quentin. *Virginia Woolf: A Biography*. New York: Mariner Books, 1974.

Bodenheimer, Rosemarie. *Knowing Dickens*. Ithaca: Cornell University Press, 2010.

Dunaway, David King. *Huxley in Hollywood*. New York: Anchor Books, 1991.

Murray, Nicholas. *Aldous Huxley: A Biography*. New York: Macmillan, 2003.

Nichols, Lewis. "Talk with Mr. Stevens." *New York Times*. October 3, 1954. www.nytimes.com/books/97/12/21/home/stevens-talk.html.

Parini, Jay. *Robert Frost: A Life*. New York: Henry Holt and Company, 1999.

Stevenson, Robert Louis. *Travels with a Donkey in the Cévannes*. Boston: Roberts Brothers, 1879.

———. "Walking Tours." *The Works of Robert Louis Stevenson*. Edited by Charles Curtis Bigelow and Temple Scott. Vol. 6. New York: Davos Press, 1906.

Thoreau, Henry David. *Walking*. Thoreau Reader. http://thoreau.eserver.org/walking.html (August 1, 2012).

Tuckerman Mason, Edward, ed. *Personal Traits of British Authors*. New York: Charles Scribner's Sons, 1885.

Zack, Wolfgang. *Literary Interrelations: Ireland, England, and the World*. Edited by Heinz Kosok. Amsterdam: John Benjamins Publishing Company, 1987.

A Mysterious Tail: Edgar Allan Poe

Allen, Hervey. *Israfel: The Life and Times of Edgar Allan Poe*. New York: Holt, Rinehart and Winston, 1960.

Poe, Edgar Allan. "Instinct Versus Reason." *The Collected Works of Edgar Allan Poe, Vol II: Tales and Sketches.* Edited by Thomas Ollive Mabbott. Cambridge: Belknap Press, 1978, pp. 477–480.

———. *Tales of Mystery and Imagination.* New York: Henry Frowde, 1903.

———. *The Unknown Poe.* Edited by Raymond Foye. San Francisco: City Light Publishers, 2001.

Silverman, Kenneth. *Edgar A. Poe: Mournful and Never-Ending Remembrance.* New York: Harper Perennial, 1992.

"Unpublished Correspondence by Edgar A. Poe." *Appletons' Journal* 4 (D. Appleton and Company, 1878), pp. 421–429.

Scrolling

Campbell, James. *This Is the Beat Generation: New York–San Francisco–Paris.* Berkeley: University of California Press, 2001.

Charters, Ann. *Kerouac: A Biography.* New York: St. Martin's Press, 1994.

Shea, Andrea. "Jack Kerouac's Famous Scroll, 'On the Road' Again." National Public Radio. July 2007. www.npr.org/templates/story/story.php?storyId=11709924.

The Traveling Desk: Charles Dickens

Bodenheimer, Rosemarie. *Knowing Dickens.* Ithaca: Cornell University Press, 2010.

Forster, John. *The Life of Charles Dickens.* Vol 2: 1847–1870. New York: Charles Scribner's Sons, 1900.

Hotten, John Camden. *Charles Dickens: The Story of His Life*. London: Woodfall and Kinder, 1873.

Keim, Albert, and Louis Lumet. *Charles Dickens*. New York: Frederick A. Stokes, 1914.

Slater, Michael. *Charles Dickens*. New Haven: Yale University Press, 2009.

Tomalin, Claire. *Charles Dickens: A Life*. New York: Penguin Press, 2011.

Quilled Muses

Gooch, Brad. *Flannery: A Life of Flannery O'Connor*. New York: Little, Brown and Company, 2009.

Hotten, John Camden. *Charles Dickens: The Story of His Life*. London: Woodfall and Kinder, 1873.

Maunder, Andrew. *The Facts on File Companion to the British Short Story*. New York: Facts on File, 2007.

Poe, Edgar Allan. *Poe: Essays and Reviews*. Edited by G. R. Thompson. New York: Library of America, 1984.

Yeats, William Butler. *The Collected Works of W. B. Yeats. Vol III: Autobiographies*. Edited by Douglas Archibald and William O'Donnell. New York: Touchstone, 1999.

Paper Topography: Edith Wharton

Benstock, Shari. *No Gifts from Chance: A Biography of Edith Wharton*. Austin: University of Texas Press, 1994.

Lee, Hermoine. *Edith Wharton*. New York: Vintage, 2008.

Wharton, Edith. *The Writing of Fiction*. New York: Scribner, 1997.

Wilson, Richard Guy, John Arthur, and Pauline C. Metcalf. *Edith Wharton at Home: Life at the Mount*. New York: Monacelli Press, 2012.

Bright-Eyed

Bradbury, Ray. *Conversations with Ray Bradbury*. Edited by Steven L. Aggelis. Jackson: University Press of Mississippi, 1994.

Goldman-Price, Irene. *My Dear Governess: The Letters of Edith Wharton to Anna Bahlmann*. New Haven: Yale University Press, 2012.

Krementz, Jill. *The Writer's Desk*. New York: Random House, 1996.

Morrison, Toni. *Conversations with Toni Morrison*. Edited by Carol C. Denard. Jackson: University Press of Mississippi, 2008.

Porter, Katherine Anne. "The Art of Fiction: No. 29." Interview by Barbara Thompson Davis. *Paris Review*, no. 29 (Winter–Spring 1963).

Stegner, Wallace. *On Teaching and Writing Fiction*. Edited by Lynn Stegner. New York: Penguin, 2002.

The Cork Shield: Marcel Proust

Albaret, Céleste. *Monsieur Proust*. Translated by Barbara Bray. New York: New York Review of Books, 2003.

Carter, William C. *Marcel Proust: A Life*. New Haven: Yale University Press, 2002.

Fuss, Diana. *A Sense of the Interior: Four Rooms and the Writers That Shaped Them*. London: Taylor & Francis, 2004.

White, Edmund. *Marcel Proust: A Life*. New York: Viking, 1999.

Flea Circus: Colette

Ackerman, Diane. "O Muse! You Do Make Things Difficult!" *New York Times.* November 12, 1989. www.nytimes.com/books/97/03/02/reviews/ackerman-poets.html.

Colette. *Earthly Paradise: An Autobiography Drawn from Her Lifetime Writings.* Edited by Robert Phelps. New York: Farrar, Straus and Giroux, 1966.

———. *Letters from Colette.* Translated by Robert Phelps. New York: Ballantine, 1980.

Mitchell, Yvonne. *Colette: A Taste for Life.* New York: Harcourt Brace Jovanovich, 1975.

Paws Between the Pages

Adams, Maureen. *Shaggy Muses: The Dogs Who Inspired Virginia Woolf, Emily Dickinson, Elizabeth Barrett Browning, Edith Wharton, and Emily Brontë.* New York: Ballantine, 2007.

Brennan, Carlene Fredericka. *Hemingway's Cats.* Foreword by Hilary Hemingway. Sarasota: Pineapple Press, 2011.

Chandler, Raymond. *Raymond Chandler Speaking.* Edited by Dorothy Gardiner and Kathrine Sorley Walker. Berkeley: University of California Press, 1977.

Dickens, Mary. *Charles Dickens, by His Eldest Daughter.* New York: Cassell & Company, 1885.

Poe, Edgar Allan. "Instinct Versus Reason." *The Collected Works of Edgar Allan Poe, Vol II: Tales and Sketches.* Edited by Thomas Ollive Mabbott. Cambridge: Belknap Press, 1978, pp. 477–480.

Rubin, Karen. "The Morgan Library Gives Access to Creative Process of Cultural Icons." Examiner.com. April 22, 2012. www

.examiner.com/article/the-morgan-library-gives-access-to
-creative-process-of-cultural-icons.

Styron, William. "Walking with Aquinnah." *Havanas in Camelot: Personal Essays*. New York: Random House, 2009.

Traffic Jamming: Gertrude Stein

Clarke, Deborah. *Driving Women: Fiction and Automobile Culture in Twentieth-Century America*. Baltimore: Johns Hopkins University Press, 2007.

Mellow, James R. *Charmed Circle: Gertrude Stein and Company*. New York: Henry Holt and Company, 2003.

Scharff, Virginia. *Taking the Wheel: Women and the Coming of the Motor Age*. Albuquerque: University of New Mexico Press, 1992.

Simon, Linda, ed. *Gertrude Stein Remembered*. Lincoln: University of Nebraska Press, 1994.

Stein, Gertrude. *The Autobiography of Alice B. Toklas*. New York: Penguin, 2001.

Toklas, Alice. *The Alice B. Toklas Cookbook*. Guilford: Lyons Press, 1998.

Wagner-Martin, Linda. *Favored Strangers: Gertrude Stein and Her Family*. New Brunswick: Rutgers University Press, 1997.

On the Move

Allen, Woody. "The Art of Humor No. 1." Interview by Michiko Kakutani. *Paris Review*, no. 136 (Fall 1995).

Halpert, Sam. *Raymond Carver: An Oral Biography*. Iowa City: University of Iowa Press, 1995.

Heller, Joseph. *Conversations with Joseph Heller.* Edited by Adam J. Sorkin. Jackson: University Press of Mississippi, 1993.

Le Carré, John. "The Art of Fiction No. 149." Interview by George Plimpton. *Paris Review,* no. 143 (Summer 1997).

Lockhart, John Gibson. *Memoirs of the Life of Sir Walter Scott, Bart.* Vol. 1. Philadelphia: Carey, Lea, and Blanchard, 1837.

"Ten Rules for Writing Fiction." *The Guardian.* February 19, 2010. www.guardian.co.uk/books/2010/feb/20/ten-rules-for-writing-fiction-part-one.

Wiesel, Elie. "The Art of Fiction No. 79." Interview by John S. Friedman. *Paris Review,* no. 91 (Spring 1984).

Tunneling by the Thousands: Jack London

Haley, James L. *Wolf: The Lives of Jack London.* New York: Basic Books, 2010.

Kershaw, Alex. *Jack London: A Life.* New York: St. Martin's Press, 1999.

Kingman, Russ. *A Pictorial Life of Jack London.* New York: Crown Publishing, 1979.

In the Shadow of Masters

Angelou, Maya. "The Art of Fiction No. 119." Interview by George Plimpton. *Paris Review,* no. 116 (Fall 1990).

Bradbury, Ray. "The Art of Fiction No. 203." Interview by Sam Weller. *Paris Review,* no. 192 (Spring 2010).

Didion, Joan. "The Art of Fiction No. 71." Interview by Linda Kuehl. *Paris Review,* no. 74 (Fall–Winter 1978).

Krementz, Jill. *The Writer's Desk.* New York: Random House, 1996.

Maugham, W. Somerset. *The Summing Up.* Garden City: Double-day, Doran & Co., 1938.

Stendhal. *The Charterhouse of Parma.* New York: Random House, 1999.

A Writer's Easel: Virginia Woolf

Bell, Quentin. *Virginia Woolf: A Biography.* New York: Mariner Books, 1974.

Curtis, Vanessa. *Virginia Woolf's Women.* Madison: University of Wisconsin Press, 2003.

Lee, Hermoine. *Virginia Woolf.* New York: Vintage, 1996.

Woolf, Virginia. *The Diary of Virginia Woolf, Vol 5: 1936–41.* Edited by Anne Olivier Bell. New York: Mariner Books, 1985.

———. *A Writer's Diary.* New York: Mariner Books, 2003.

Board Writing

Frost, Robert. "The Art of Poetry No. 2." Interview by Richard Poirier. *Paris Review,* no. 24 (Summer–Fall 1960).

Sturrock, Donald. *Storyteller: The Authorized Biography of Roald Dahl.* New York: Simon and Schuster, 2010.

Walker, Alice. *Langston Hughes: American Poet.* New York: Amistad, 2005.

The Full Spectrum

Blotner, Joseph. *Faulkner: A Biography.* New York: Vintage, 1991.

Kipling, Rudyard. *A Sussex Kipling: An Anthology of Poetry and Prose.* Sussex: Pomegranate Press, 2007.

Reif, Rita. "Following the Wonderful Logic of 'Wonderland." *New York Times.* November 15, 1998. www.nytimes.com/1998/11/15/books/art-architecture-following-the-wonderful-logic-of-wonderland.html.

Crayon, Scissors, and Paste: James Joyce

Beach, Sylvia. *Shakespeare and Company.* 2nd ed. Lincoln: Bison Books, 1991.

Bowker, Gordon. *James Joyce: A New Biography.* New York: Farrar, Straus and Giroux, 2012.

Colum, Mary, and Padraic Colum. *Our Friend James Joyce.* London: Victor Gollancz, 1959.

Coyle, John. *James Joyce: Ulysses/A Portrait of the Artist as a Young Man.* West Sussex: Columbia University Press, 1998.

Ellmann, Richard. *James Joyce.* Rev. ed. New York: Oxford University Press, 1983.

Joyce, James. *Letters of James Joyce.* Vol. 3. Edited by Richard Ellmann. London: Faber and Faber, 1966.

Litz, A. Walton. *The Art of James Joyce: Method and Design in* Ulysses *and* Finnegans Wake. London: Oxford University Press, 1961.

Lyons, J. B. *James Joyce and Medicine.* New York: Humanities Press, 1974.

Cigarettes, Twins, and the Evil Eye

Bowker, Gordon. *James Joyce: A New Biography.* New York: Farrar, Straus and Giroux, 2012.

Ellmann, Richard. *James Joyce.* Rev. ed. New York: Oxford University Press, 1983.

Freedman, Carl. *Conversations with Isaac Asimov.* Jackson: University Press of Mississippi, 2005.

Inge, M. Thomas. *Truman Capote: Conversations.* Jackson: University Press of Mississippi, 1987.

Kerouac, Jack. "The Art of Fiction No. 41." Interview by Ted Berrigan. *Paris Review,* no. 43 (Summer 1968).

Lyons, Leonard. "Maugham Battles the Evil Eye and So Far the Charm Is Fine." *Lawrence Journal-World.* March 10, 1965, p. 4.

Maugham, W. Somerset. *The Summing Up.* Garden City: Doubleday, Doran & Co., 1938.

Sheehan, Edward R. F. "Evelyn Waugh Runs a Fair." *Harper's Magazine.* January 1960, pp. 30–37.

Leafing Through the Pages: D. H. Lawrence

Brett, Dorothy. *Lawrence and Brett: A Friendship.* Sante Fe: Sunstone Press, 2006.

Flanner, Janet. *Paris Was Yesterday: 1925–1939.* Edited by Irving Drutman. New York: Mariner Books, 1988.

Kinkead-Weekes, Mark. *D. H. Lawrence: Triumph to Exile 1912–1922.* Cambridge: Cambridge University Press, 1996.

Lawrence, D. H. *The Letters of D. H. Lawrence.* Edited by Warren Roberts, James T. Boulton, and Elizabeth Mansfield. Cambridge: Cambridge University Press, 2002.

Moore, Harry T. *The Priest of Love: The Life of D. H. Lawrence.* New York: Penguin Books, 1981.

Nin, Anaïs. *D. H. Lawrence: An Unprofessional Study.* Paris: Black Manikin Press, 1932.

Sagar, Keith. *D. H. Lawrence: A Calendar of His Works.* Manchester: Manchester University Press, 1979.

When in Doubt . . .

King, Stephen. "Cannibals, The." StephenKing.com. September 1, 2012. www.stephenking.com/library/unpublished/canni bals_the.html.

Kois, Dan. "Why Do Writers Abandon Novels?" *New York Times.* March 2011. www.nytimes.com/2011/03/06/books/review/ Kois-t.html.

Page, Norman, ed. *Oxford Reader's Companion to Hardy.* Oxford: Oxford University Press, 2000.

Shields, Charles J. *Mockingbird: A Portrait of Harper Lee.* New York: Henry Holt and Company, 2007.

Puzzling Assembly: Vladimir Nabokov

Boyd, Brian. *Vladimir Nabokov: The American Years.* Princeton: Princeton University Press, 1993.

Field, Andrew. *VN: The Life and Art of Vladimir Nabokov.* New York: Crown Publishing, 1977.

Nabokov, Vladimir. "The Art of Fiction No. 40." Interview by Herbert Gold. *Paris Review,* no. 41 (Summer–Fall 1967).

———. "Playboy Interview: Vladimir Nabokov." Interview by Alvin Toffler. *Playboy.* January 1964, pp. 35–45.

Bath Time

Adler, David A. *B. Franklin, Printer.* New York: Holiday House, 2001.

Alter, Alexandra. "How to Write a Great Novel." *Wall Street Journal.* November 13, 2009. http://online.wsj.com/article/SB1000142 40527487037400045745134631060120106.html.

Berg, Rona. "Beauty: Sense and Sensuality." *New York Times Magazine.* May 3, 1992. www.nytimes.com/1992/05/03/magazine/ beauty-sense-and-sensuality.html.

Boyd, Brian. *Vladimir Nabokov: The American Years.* Princeton: Princeton University Press, 1993.

Dennis, Nigel. "Genteel Queen of Crime." *Life.* May 14, 1956, pp. 87–102.

Field, Andrew. *VN: The Life and Art of Vladimir Nabokov.* New York: Crown Publishing, 1977.

Hegermann-Lindencrone, Madame de. "A Diplomat's Wife in Paris." *Harper's Magazine.* June–November, 1914, pp. 763–774.

Meyers, Jeffrey. *Somerset Maugham: A Life.* New York: Vintage, 2005.

Nabokov, Vladimir. "Playboy Interview: Vladimir Nabokov." Interview by Alvin Toffler. *Playboy.* January 1964, pp. 35–45.

Silverstein, Stuart Y. *Not Much Fun: The Lost Poems of Dorothy Parker.* New York: Simon and Schuster, 2009.

Outstanding Prose: Ernest Hemingway

Hemingway, Ernest. *Conversations with Ernest Hemingway.* Jackson: University Press of Mississippi, 1986.

———. *Selected Letters 1917–1961.* Edited by Carlos Baker. New York: Scribner, 2003.

Lynn, Kenneth S. *Hemingway.* Cambridge: Harvard University Press, 1995.

Mellow, James R. *Hemingway: A Life Without Consequences*. Cambridge: Da Capo Press, 1993.

Meyers, Jeffrey. *Hemingway: A Biography*. Cambridge: Da Capo Press, 1999.

"The Photographic Essay: Hemingway." *Life*. July 14, 1961, pp. 59–70.

Reynolds, Michael. *Hemingway: The 1930s Through the Final Years*. New York: W. W. Norton and Company, 2012.

Sound Writing: John Steinbeck

Benson, Jackson J. *The True Adventures of John Steinbeck, Writer*. New York: Viking, 1984.

Fensch, Thomas, ed. *Conversations with John Steinbeck*. Jackson: University Press of Mississippi, 1988.

Parini, Jay. *John Steinbeck: A Biography*. New York: Henry Holt and Company, 1995.

Scott, Robert. "The Work Habits of Highly Successful Writers." *Writer's Digest*. May 2005, pp. 33–37.

Simmond, Roy. "The Composition, Publication, and Reception of John Steinbeck's *The Wayward Bus*, with Biographical Background: Chapter Two: 'New York Is a Wonderful City': January–April 1946." *Steinbeck Review* 8, no. 2 (2011): 11–29.

Steinbeck, John. *Journal of a Novel: The East of Eden Letters*. New York: Penguin Books, 1990.

———. *Steinbeck: A Life in Letters*. Edited by Elaine Steinbeck and Robert Wallsten. New York: Penguin Books, 1989.

Speak Up

Dobranski, Stephen B. *The Cambridge Companion to Milton*. Cambridge: Cambridge University Press, 2012.

Hardyment, Christina. *Literary Trails: British Writers in Their Landscapes*. New York: Harry N. Abrams, 2000.

Lantz, Kenneth. *The Dostoevsky Encyclopedia*. Westport: Greenwood Press, 2004.

Thackeray, William Makepeace. *The Works of William Makepeace Thackeray*. Vol 12. New York: Harper & Brothers Publishers, 1898.

Pin It Down: Eudora Welty

Marrs, Suzanne. *Eudora Welty: A Biography*. New York: Houghton Mifflin Harcourt, 2006.

Marrs, Suzanne, ed. *What There Is to Say We Have Said: The Correspondence of Eudora Welty and William Maxwell*. New York: Houghton Mifflin Harcourt, 2011.

Welty, Eudora. *Conversations with Eudora Welty*. Edited by Peggy Whitman Prenshaw. Jackson: University Press of Mississippi, 1984.

———. *More Conversations with Eudora Welty*. Edited by Peggy Whitman Prenshaw. Jackson: University Press of Mississippi, 1996.

Point of View

Ackerman, Diane. "O Muse! You Do Make Things Difficult!" *New York Times*. November 12, 1989. www.nytimes.com/books/97/03/02/reviews/ackerman-poets.html.

Angelou, Maya. "The Art of Fiction No. 119." Interview by George Plimpton. *Paris Review*, no. 116 (Fall 1990).

Elliot, Jeffrey M. *Conversations with Maya Angelou.* Jackson: University Press of Mississippi, 1989.

Hemingway, Ernest. "The Art of Fiction No. 21." Interview by George Plimpton. *Paris Review*, no. 18 (Spring 1958).

Paine, Albert Bigelow. *Mark Twain, a Biography, Volume 1, Part 1: 1835–1866.* New York: Harper and Brothers Publishers, 1912.

Steinbeck, John. *Steinbeck: A Life in Letters.* Edited by Elaine Steinbeck and Robert Wallsten. New York: Penguin Books, 1989.

"Writers' Rooms: George Bernard Shaw." May 30, 2008. *The Guardian.* www.guardian.co.uk/books/2008/may/30/writers.rooms.george.bernard.shaw.

Don't Get Up: Truman Capote

Capote, Truman. "The Art of Fiction No. 17." Interview by Pati Hill. *Paris Review*, no. 16 (Spring–Summer 1957).

———. *Truman Capote: Conversations.* Edited by M. Thomas Inge. Jackson: University Press of Mississippi, 1987.

Clarke, Gerald. *Capote: A Biography.* New York: Carroll & Graf, 2001.

Plimpton, George. *Truman Capote: In Which Various Friends, Enemies, Acquaintances and Detractors Recall His Turbulent Career.* New York: Anchor Books, 1998.

Off the Recorder

Clarke, Gerald. *Capote: A Biography.* New York: Carroll & Graf, 2001.

Hibbard, Allen. *Conversations with William S. Burroughs.* Jackson: University Press of Mississippi, 2000.

Talese, Gay. "How the Tape Recorder Killed Journalism." Interview by Big Think. http://bigthink.com/ideas/16545. September 28, 2009.

Early to Write: Flannery O'Connor

Gooch, Brad. *Flannery: A Life of Flannery O'Connor.* New York: Little, Brown and Company, 2009.

Magee, Rosemary M., ed. *Conversations with Flannery O'Connor.* Jackson: University Press of Mississippi, 1987.

O'Connor, Flannery. *The Habit of Being: Letters of Flannery O'Connor.* Edited by Sally Fitzgerald. New York: Farrar, Straus and Giroux, 1988.

Sweet Teeth

Gooch, Brad. *Flannery: A Life of Flannery O'Connor.* New York: Little, Brown and Company, 2009.

Halpert, Sam. *Raymond Carver: An Oral Biography.* Iowa City: University of Iowa Press, 1995.

Kauffmann, Stanley. "Remembering Ray." *New Republic.* June 7, 2012. www.tnr.com/blog/plank/103934/remembering-ray-bradbury-fahrenheit-kauffmann.

O'Connor, Flannery. *The Habit of Being: Letters of Flannery O'Connor.* Edited by Sally Fitzgerald. New York: Farrar, Straus and Giroux, 1988.

Sklenicka, Carol. *Raymond Carver: A Writer's Life.* New York: Scribner, 2009.

Index

About the Author

Celia Blue Johnson graduated from New York University with a master's degree in English and American literature, and went on to edit fiction and nonfiction at major publishing houses. She is the creative director of Slice Literary, a Brooklyn-based nonprofit organization that has been featured in the *New Yorker*, the *New York Times*, and *Poets & Writers*. Celia is also the author of *Dancing with Mrs. Dalloway: Stories of the Inspiration Behind Great Works of Literature*. She lives with her husband and daughter in Portland, Maine.